Sew
Baby Doll
Clothes

Joan Hinds

©2005 Joan Hinds
Published by

kp books
An Imprint of F+W Publications

700 East State Street • Iola, WI 54990-0001
715-445-2214 • 888-457-2873

Our toll-free number to place an order or obtain
a free catalog is (800) 258-0929.

Dolls pictured on the cover (from left to right): Bitty Twins® by Pleasant Company and Götz®.
Dolls pictured on the title page: Adora Doll®

The following registered trademark terms and companies appear in this publication:
Adora Doll®, Berenguer®, Bitty Baby®, Bitty Twins®, Chenille by the Yard™, Corolle™,
Dritz for Dolls®, Fisher-Price®, Götz®, Velcro® and Zapf Creation®.

Library of Congress Catalog Number: 2004115350

ISBN: 0-87349-934-4

Designed by Emily Adler
Edited by Sarah Herman

Printed in the United States of America

Dedication

To baby doll lovers of all ages.

Acknowledgments

Many, many thanks go to the talented and creative people who helped me with the design and completion of this book! It truly has been a group effort!

My dear friends Marilee Sagat, Lauri Cushing, Ceci Riehl and Audrey Finch, who helped with many projects, especially the knitted and embroidered clothing. You also helped me weather the rough spots this year.

My terrific illustrator, Kathy Marsaa, who makes my instructions come to life with her drawings.

The enthusiastic staff at KP Books, including Julie, Barbara, Sarah and photographers Kris and Bob, who are all wonderful to work with.

Lastly, to my husband Fletcher, who patiently offers design and technical assistance whenever I need his help.

Table of Contents

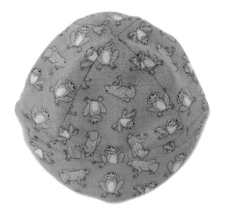

Introduction

GÖTZ

Often one of the first toys a child receives is a special baby doll. Many of us remember that special doll. Others receive a baby doll as an older child. Sometimes, as adults, we will purchase a beautiful baby doll that "speaks" to us. Regardless of the way we have acquired them, baby dolls need wardrobes with all the essentials.

I have designed 12 books of clothing patterns for the popular 18-inch child doll. Interest in baby dolls has increased, so I have designed this book with patterns to fit them. The patterns in this book fit baby dolls from 12" to 22". Acquiring dolls to model the new clothing was lots of fun. There are many wonderful vinyl baby dolls on the market today that come in different price ranges. I have tried to include both "collector" dolls and "everyday" dolls in this pattern book.

The outfits featured in this book range from a classic baby doll layette to modern fleece clothing. It also includes the basics: bib overalls and dresses. I have included several outfits that are matching boy and girl fashions for the twin dolls that are very popular today. Please note that some of the twin garments, such as bib overalls or coveralls, can be worn by girl dolls, too. Some of the clothing is suitable for very young-looking baby dolls, while other outfits may be more suitable for toddler dolls.

Whether you are sewing baby doll clothes for a very special young child or for your own collector doll, these patterns will help you make beautiful baby doll clothing that you will treasure for years to come.

Which Dolls Will These Patterns Fit?

The patterns in this book are sized to fit 12" to 22" baby dolls with categories for sizes small, medium, large and extra large. With such a large size range, I could not possibly fit patterns to every baby doll on the market, so I had to pick representatives for each category. I was then able to come up with a range of measurements for each size.

So how will you know which size your doll wears? First, you need to measure your doll. As a former hospital nursery nurse, I have had plenty of opportunities to measure babies. The way to measure the length of a crying, slippery newborn infant (while wearing gloves) is to lay the baby over a tape measure. The tape measure should be flush with the top of the baby's head. The knee is held down to extend the leg and a mark is made at the bottom of the heel. This method works well for baby dolls as well. Place your doll on a flat surface over a tape measure that begins just at the top of the head. Hold the knee down as best as you can and mark the heel. This will give you the height of your doll. This method is much easier than holding the doll upright in one hand, and measuring with the other.

The measurement you get may not always match the height listed by the manufacturer. In fact, it will sometimes be way off. I finally figured out that some doll companies measure to the heel of the doll, while others continue beyond the heel and include the whole length of the foot in the measurement. This is probably done because baby doll legs often have the foot bent at the ankle, since the doll will not be standing. For example, one manufacturer will call a doll 15" tall, but another will call it 16.5" tall because the foot length is included. Use my method of measuring your doll's height for the patterns in this book.

The next step is to take a full set of measurements. The best way to measure small baby doll parts is to use a narrow tape measure. The measurements should include the height, chest, waist, hip, shoulder width and arm and leg length. You also need to measure the circumference of the wrist, ankle, upper arm, upper leg and head. To measure the height, use my technique described at left. To measure the arm length, hold the end of the tape measure under the arm and measure along the inside of the arm. Be sure to curve the tape measure if the arm is bent. The leg length is measured like the inseam of pants, by measuring from the crotch to the ankle. Compare your measurements to the range of measurements in each size category. The most important measurements are the neck circumference, waist and shoulder width. You should choose the size category closest to these measurements.

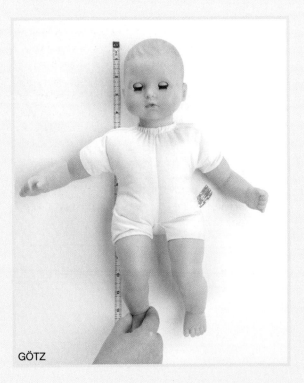

GÖTZ

	Small	Medium	Large	X-Large
Height	12"-13"*	14"-16"**	17"-19"***	20"-22"****
Head	10½"-11"	12"-13"	13"-13½"	14½"- 15¾"
Neck	5½"-6"	6¼"-7"	6½"-8"	8"-9"
Chest	9½"-9¾"	12"-12¼"	13"-15"	15"-16"
Waist	9¾"-10¼"	11½"-12"	15"-16"	15"-16"
Arm Length	3½"-4"	4"- 4¼"	5"-5¼"	5¾"-6½"
Upper Arm Circumference	3½"-4½"	4¾"-5"	5"-6"	6"-6¾"
Wrist	3"-3½"	3½"-3¾"	3¾"-4¼"	4¼"- 4½"
Leg Length	3½"-4"	5"-5½"	5"-5½"	6"-7"
Upper Leg Circumference	5¼"-5½"	6¾"-7"	6½"-7½"	8"-9"
Ankle	3¼"-3½"	4¼"-4½"	4½"-5"	4½"-5¼"

* Includes Götz Muffin, Corolle Cailin and Zapf Creation dolls.
** Includes Bitty Baby and Bitty Twins by Pleasant Company, Lee Middleton, Corolle, Götz Maxi-Muffin and Götz baby dolls.
*** Includes Adora Doll, Corolle and Zapf Creation dolls. Dolls in this category may be listed by manufacturer as 20" tall because foot length was included in the height.
**** Includes Adora Doll, Zapf Creation and Berenguer dolls.

Once you have compared measurements, you may find that your doll does not fit entirely in one category. That was the case with several dolls I used for models. For example, the doll shown in the top with ruffled hem and beret on page 32 wears a size large, except for one measurement. Her arms are 2" shorter than the other dolls in that category, so I had to shorten the arm length of her clothing. The doll wearing the christening gown on page 108 wears a size medium, except for longer arm and leg lengths; I had to make the sleeves longer in this case. The coveralls shown on the dolls on page 24 are size medium. The head circumference for each doll, however, falls in the size small category, so I used size small for their caps. Please note that these adjustments were made after the patterns were drafted, so each pattern piece was drawn according to the measurements listed above. You can make similar adjustments if you lengthen or shorten the sleeves or pant leg, or overlap the back opening a little more or a little less.

Now that you have decided which size to make for your doll, you will have to find the pattern pieces for each outfit and follow the instructions in the book. The instructions for each outfit include all the sizes in the text. The first measurement listed is always for the size small. The subsequent measurements in parentheses for the other sizes will always be listed in the same increasing order. For example, elastic length may be listed as follows: 3" (4", 5", 6"). This means that you will cut 3" of elastic for size small. The next measurement in parentheses is for size medium. For this size you will cut 4" of elastic. The next measurement, for size large, is 5". Finally, size x-large is 6". This will be true for all the instructions regardless of what size the model wears.

Small	Medium	Large	X-Large
⇧	⇧	⇧	⇧
3"	(4",	5",	6")

Getting Started

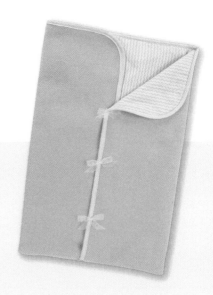

You have chosen the outfit you want to make, have found the pattern pieces in your doll's size, and are anxious to begin. A few words about general sewing instructions are needed. Please read this section carefully before you begin.

Gather all your equipment. Begin with a sewing machine, sewing shears, pins, seam gauge, narrow tape measure and washout marker. A serger is not necessary, even for the knit garments, but it helps with construction and gives seam allowances a clean finish. A steam iron is a must. There is a "mini-iron" designed for the quilting industry that is also perfect for the small areas in doll clothing construction. Small doll-sized ironing boards are essential for pressing small sleeves, collars, pant legs, etc. A bias tape maker may be helpful to create your own custom bias bindings for clothing, blankets and quilts.

Choosing fabric is always my favorite part of sewing for dolls. Baby doll clothing lends itself to soft fabrics, especially knits and fleece. Fleece fabrics are very plentiful in most fabric stores. Look for small-sized prints and "micro fleece," which is much thinner. Knits may be harder to find. There are many Internet sources for knit prints and solids if you are unable to find them in stores. For woven fabrics, don't overlook the quilting cottons. You can find many juvenile or baby-themed prints that work well for doll clothing. Often the design in the fabric print will dictate its use. The gingerbread print for the outfits on page 100 was perfect for holiday clothes. The party balloon print in the dress on page 92 was just right for a birthday outfit. Flannel is often printed with babies in mind, so be sure to check it out. With woven fabrics, be sure that you choose a lighter-weight fabric. If you want to use denim, for instance, choose a thin denim or even chambray so your garments will drape properly.

Please note that all seam allowances are ¼" unless specified otherwise. We have become accustomed to using ⅝" seam allowance for garment sewing, so the transition to narrower seams may take a little effort. Some of us tend to make the seams slightly wider than ¼". This may affect the fit. An easy way to ensure you have accurate seam allowances is to use a quilting presser foot that has a width of ¼" built in. Be aware that the foot has a small hole, so you cannot zigzag stitch without switching presser feet. Another option is to use an edge-stitching foot. If your sewing machine can adjust the needle position from side-to-side, you can move the needle so that the stitching will be exactly ¼" from the fabric edge.

Seam finishes are only mentioned when absolutely necessary. Feel free to finish the seam allowances as you prefer, either with a serger or zigzag stitching. Some machines have a three-step zigzag, which allows the fabric to be stitched without rolling or bunching. I have used Velcro strips for closures on most of the garments in this book, but you can substitute snaps if you prefer.

Embellishments for baby doll clothing are the icing on the cake. I have included many garments that have machine embroidery, decorative stitching, appliqué and even hand embroidery. Please note many of the techniques are interchangeable. You may want to make the dress with the hand embroidered gingerbread collar, but want to use a machine embroidery design instead. Or perhaps you want to substitute the machine embroidery on the coveralls with the felt appliqué shown on the pajamas or denim jumper. Feel free to use your creativity to create your own unique doll clothing.

Making Sweaters and Other Hand Knits For Dolls

Knitted garments and blankets are wonderful additions to add to your doll's wardrobe. Instructions for two sweaters, two caps, booties, and a blanket are included in this book. The sweater with cap and booties, made with pastel colors, has a butterfly border. The other sweater and cap with a checkerboard border and stripes are done in brighter primary colors. This sweater outfit is suitable for toddler boy and girl dolls.

Before you begin knitting, familiarize yourself with a few general terms and guidelines for knitting the patterns in this book. They are as follows:

Bind off and join: This is an easy and neat way to finish the shoulder seam. Line up both points of the needle with the stitches to be bound off, so the front and back of the sweater are on top of each other, outsides together. Using a second needle or a crochet hook and the working yarn, or 24" tail that is hanging there, bring a loop through the last loop on both needles. That is, insert the hook or needle as if to knit into the last loop on the front needle and then the last loop on the back needle and pull the loop through both. Pull one stitch off each needle. Repeat this step with the next two stitches. Now pull the first stitch on the right hand needle over the second, or if using a crochet hook, pull the second stitch through the first. Give this stitch an extra tug to be sure it doesn't get too tight. Continue in this manner until all stitches from the front shoulder have been used up.

CO: Cast on.

K1, p1 rib: On the outside repeat (k1, p1) across. On the inside knit the knits and purl the purls.

K2, p2 rib: On the outside repeat (k2, p2) across. On the inside knit the knits and purl the purls.

K2 tog: Knit two stitches together as one. (A decrease slanting right.)

Knit the knits and purl the purls: On the inside of the work a stitch that was knitted on the outside looks like a purl. If you purl this stitch on the inside it will look like a knit stitch on the outside. This term means work the opposite stitch on the inside so that from the outside it looks the same as the stitch below it. A confusing way of stating something very simple.

M1: (Make one) Insert left needle, from front to back, under the horizontal strand between last stitch worked and next stitch on left needle, forming a loop on needle. Knit through the back of this loop.

Pick up and knit: Insert right needle into edge of work under one or two firm strands; wrap yarn around needle as if to knit and pull loop through, creating a new loop on left needle.

Pm: Place a stitch marker on the needle.

Psso: Pass slipped stitch over the stitch immediately left of it on the right hand needle and drop it. (A decrease slanting left.)

Seed stitch: This stitch is good for borders, because it doesn't roll at the edge. Looking at the work from the outside, you have a checkerboard pattern of purls and knits. Over an even number of stitches, k1, p1 on the outside; p1, k1 on the inside. Over an odd number of stitches, k1, p1 across on the outside; k1, p1 across on the inside. (Or knit the *purls* and purl the *knits*.) When working in the round k1, p1 across on the first row; p1, k1 across on the second, etc.

Sk2po: Slip one stitch, knit 2, pass slipped stitch over last one on needle. (3 stitches decreased to 1.)

Ssk: (Slip, slip, knit) Slip two stitches, one at a time as if to knit; Slide left needle through the front loops of these slipped stitches, from left to right, and knit them together from this position. (A decrease slanting left.)

St(s): Stitch(es).

Stockinette stitch: Knit all stitches on the outside. Purl all stitches on the inside. When knitting in the round knit all rounds.

W&T: Wrap and turn. Bring yarn to front of work. Slip one stitch. Bring yarn to back of work. Slip the stitch back to the left needle. Turn. This eliminates a hole at the turning point.

Yo: (Yarn over) Pass yarn over needle as if to knit. (1 stitch added which will create a hole.)

Baby Doll Layette

BITTY BABY BY PLEASANT COMPANY

Often the first wardrobe for baby dolls is a classic layette. The simply-constructed pieces are usually sewn from flannel. This layette features a front opening top (called a diaper shirt) paired with elastic-leg panties (called a diaper cover). The one-piece bonnet has a drawstring at the back of the head to give it a rounded shape. It can be made without the lace at the face opening if you are sewing for a boy baby doll. A bib to match the layette is trimmed with the same flannel bias binding. The booties are also one piece with a seam on the bottom of the foot. You can decorate the top of the booties in many different ways, including ribbon bows or flowers, or novelty button shapes. Try making an animal face with button eyes and nose, and felt "ears" stitched on the cuff!

DIAPER COVER, DIAPER SHIRT, BONNET AND BOOTIES

SUPPLIES

¼ yd. (¼ yd., ½ yd., ½ yd.) print flannel

¼ yd. (¼ yd., ⅓ yd., ⅓ yd.) pink flannel

1 yd. (1¼ yd., 1½ yd., 1½ yd.) bias strip of pink gingham for the binding, 2" wide

2 small Velcro circles

1 yd. pink iridescent ribbon, ½" wide

8" (11", 14", 17") elastic for the waist, ⅜" wide

10½" (12", 14", 16") elastic for the leg openings, ⅛" wide

6½" (9", 10", 11") elastic for the booties, ⅛" wide

½ yd. satin ribbon for the back opening of the bonnet, ⅛" wide

⅔ yd. gingham ribbon for the bonnet ties, ⅝" (⅞", ⅞", ⅞") wide

9" (12", 12", 15") pre-gathered eyelet lace, 1" (1½", 1½", 1½") wide

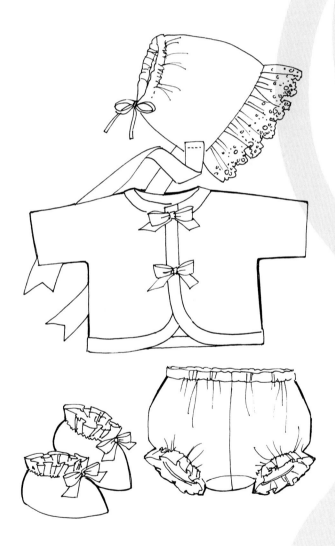

CUTTING INSTRUCTIONS

From the print flannel, cut:
- Two shirt fronts (Pattern 1).
- One shirt back (Pattern 2).
- Two booties (Pattern 4).
- One bonnet (Pattern 5).

From the pink flannel, cut:
- Four diaper covers (Pattern 7).

DIAPER COVER DIAPER SHIRT

1 With right sides together, sew the center front and center back seams of the diaper covers. Sew the side seams with right sides together.

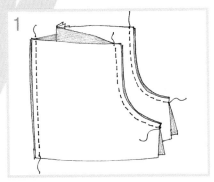

2 Narrow-hem the lower edges of the diaper cover. Cut the leg opening elastic in half. Starting at one side of the leg openings and ½" from the hemmed edge, sew the elastic by zigzag stitching over the top, stretching the elastic to the other side. Do not catch the elastic in your stitching except to secure the ends at each side.

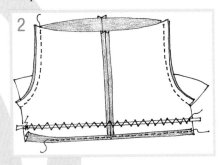

3 Sew the inner leg seam.

4 Serge or zigzag stitch the top edge of the diaper cover. Press this edge ¾" to the wrong side and stitch ½" from the folded edge, leaving a small opening in the back. Thread the waistband elastic through this casing and secure the ends. Stitch the opening closed.

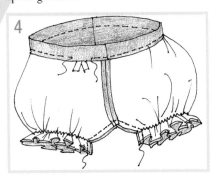

1 Sew the back to the fronts at the shoulder seams. Press the seams toward the back.

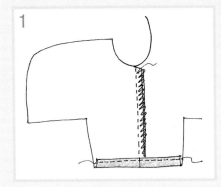

2 Serge or zigzag stitch the sleeve edges and press ½" to the wrong side. Stitch.

3 With right sides together, sew the underarm seam from the wrist to the lower edge.

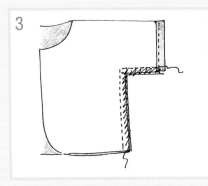

4 Press the edges of the bias strip ½" to the wrong side, or use a bias tape maker. Cut a piece long enough to bind the neckline. Open out one side of the tape and stitch to the wrong side of the neckline. Fold the binding over to the right side and topstitch, tucking in the short ends at the neckline.

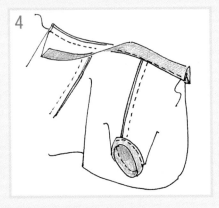

5 Using the same technique as in the previous step, stitch the bias binding to the center front and lower edges, tucking in the short ends at the neckline.

6 Stitch a Velcro circle to the neck edge of the bias binding on the front. Sew the second Velcro circle to the bias binding approximately halfway down the front opening.

7 Cut the iridescent ribbon in four equal pieces and tie two pieces into bows (the remainder will be applied to the booties). Tack each one over the Velcro circles.

Make a full-length diaper shirt, called a kimono. Use the same patterns (Patterns 1 and 2), but cut along the Kimono cutting line.

BONNET

1 Press the sides of the bonnet ¼" to the wrong side. Press another ¼" and stitch.

2 Press the long curved edge of the bonnet ¼" to the wrong side. Press another ½" and stitch to form a casing.

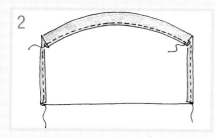

3 Pin the eyelet lace edging to the front of the bonnet with right sides together. Turn the raw ends of the lace edging to the wrong side so they are flush with the side edges of the bonnet and stitch ¼" below the casing of the eyelet. Cut off the casing and finish the seam allowance with a serger or zigzag stitch. Fold the seam allowance to the wrong side so the eyelet edging extends beyond the seam line. Topstitch a scant ⅛" from the seam line on the bonnet.

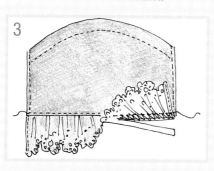

4 Cut the gingham ribbon in half. Fold one edge on each piece ½" to the wrong side and stitch at an angle to the side front edges.

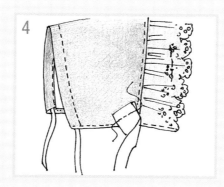

5 Thread the ⅛" ribbon through the casing and stitch the ribbon at the center of the casing to secure. Try the bonnet on the baby doll and tie the ribbon at the back of the head.

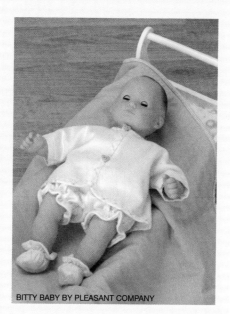

BITTY BABY BY PLEASANT COMPANY

Use solid-color flannel with print flannel bias binding for a more tailored look.

BOOTIES

1 Press the long straight edge of the booties ¼" to the wrong side. Press another ¼" and stitch.

2 Cut the elastic for the booties in half. Starting at one side of the bootie and ½" from the hemmed edge, sew the elastic by zigzag stitching over the top, stretching the elastic to the other side. Do not catch the elastic in your stitching except to secure the ends at each side.

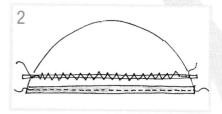

3 Fold the bootie in half with right sides together and stitch. Turn to the right side.

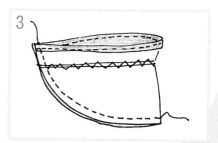

4 Tie a bow with the remaining pieces of iridescent ribbon and tack them to the front of the bootie on top of the elastic.

BIB

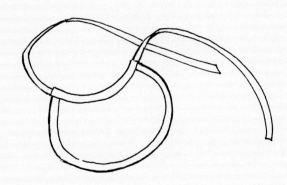

1 Press the bias binding edges ½" to the wrong side, or use a bias tape maker. Open out one of the pressed edges and stitch the right side of the bias strip to the wrong side of the outside edge of the bib. Fold the bias over to the right side and top stitch.

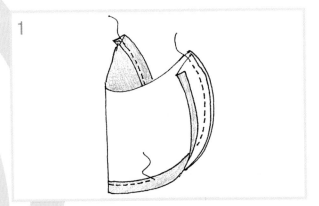

2 Cut the ribbon in half. Stitch the right side of the remaining bias binding to the wrong side of the neckline of the bib, extending each end ¼". Fold over to the right side and topstitch, enclosing the short ends and inserting a piece of the ribbon for the ties.

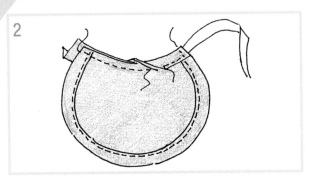

SUPPLIES

6" x 7" piece of yellow flannel

½ yd. bias strip of print flannel, 2" wide, for the binding, or double fold bias tape

20" ribbon for the ties, ¼" wide

CUTTING INSTRUCTIONS

From the yellow flannel, cut:
- One bib (Pattern 6).

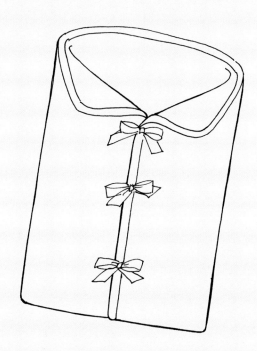

BUNTING

1 With right sides together, sew the cotton print to the fleece fabric along the two short sides and one long edge. Clip the corners; turn to the right side and press.

2 Press the long edges of the bias strip ½" to the wrong side, or use a bias tape maker. Open out one of the sides of the bias strip and stitch the right side of the strip to the lining side of the bunting. Turning the raw end ¼" to the wrong side, begin stitching 7" below the top of one of the short sides of the of the fabric rectangle. Continue across the long edge and down the remaining short side. (The raw edges of the other long side are unstitched.) Fold the bias strip to the right side of the bunting and topstitch.

3 Fold the short sides to the center, overlapping 2" with the lining side out. The side with the bias binding along the entire edge is folded first to the inside. Stitch the bottom seam. Finish the seam with a serger or zigzag stitch. Turn right-side out.

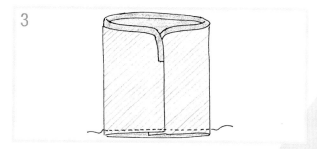

4 Sew the Velcro circles to the opening of the bunting. Stitch the first 7½" from the top, the second 4½" from the first, and the third 4" from the bottom.

5 Cut the ribbon into thirds. Tie three bows and tack them over the Velcro.

SUPPLIES

⅔ yd. fleece

⅔ yd. cotton print fabric for the lining

2 yd. bias strip of gingham fabric for the binding, 2" wide

3 Velcro circles

1 yd. iridescent ribbon, ½" wide

CUTTING INSTRUCTIONS

From the fleece, cut:

•One 22" x 31" rectangle, rounding the corners.

From the cotton print, cut:

•One 22" x 31" rectangle, rounding the corners.

Sailing Away

These toddler dolls are having loads of fun playing in their classic clothing. The shortalls for boys, worn with a T-shirt, have been updated with a machine embroidered sailboat on the front. You can choose to eliminate the embroidery or stitch a simple appliqué instead. The girl's dress has three pleats in the front and a contrasting collar and cuffs. It is decorated with simple ribbon daisies with button centers. Her quick and easy felt shoes can be made to match any outfit.

SHORT-SLEEVED T-SHIRT, SHORTALLS AND CAP

SUPPLIES

¼ yd. white knit fabric

1½" x 6½" (7½", 9", 9½") white ribbing

⅓ yd.(⅓ yd., ½ yd., ½ yd.) plaid or gingham fabric for the shortalls and cap

2" (3", 4", 4") Velcro strip

2 small snaps

2 buttons, size ¼" (¼", ½", ½")

Sailboat embroidery design*

40 wt. embroidery thread

Tear-away stabilizer

Scrap of medium-weight interfacing for the hat brim

Package of bias tape to match the color of the hat

1½"-2" elastic, ⅛" wide (optional)

*Used in this project: "Me and My Doll Clothes" by Joan Hinds by VSM Sewing, Inc.

CUTTING INSTRUCTIONS

From the white knit fabric, cut:
- One shirt front (Pattern 9).
- Two shirt backs (Pattern 10).
- Two shirt sleeves (Pattern 25).

From the plaid or gingham fabric, cut:
- One shortall front facing (Pattern 11).
- One shortall back (Pattern 12).
- One shortall back facing (Pattern 12).
- Four cap sections (Pattern 14).
- Two cap brims (Pattern 15).
- *Note:* Leave enough fabric to fit in your embroidery hoop for the front (Pattern 11).

From the interfacing, cut:
- One cap brim (Pattern 15).

SHORT-SLEEVED T-SHIRT

BITTY TWIN BY PLEASANT COMPANY

1 Press the center back edges ¼" to the wrong side and stitch.

2 With right sides together, sew the shoulder seams with a serger or zigzag stitch.

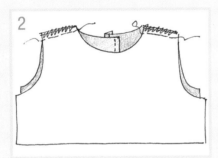

3 Fold the ribbing in half lengthwise with right sides together. Stitch the short ends and turn to the right side. Stretching the ribbing to fit the neckline, serge or zigzag stitch the ribbing to the neckline.

4 Serge or zigzag stitch the lower edges of the sleeves. Press ¼" to the wrong side and topstitch. With right sides together, serge or zigzag stitch the sleeves to the shirt armholes, easing as necessary. Serge or zigzag stitch the underarm seam, starting at the sleeve hem and finishing at the lower edge of the shirt.

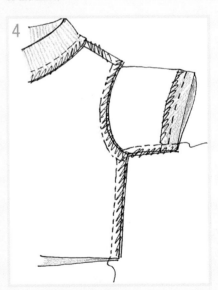

5 Serge or zigzag stitch the lower edge of the shirt. Press the edge ⅜" to the wrong side and topstitch.

6 Lapping right over left, sew the Velcro to the back opening.

1 To embroider the front of the shortall, cut a piece of plaid or gingham fabric large enough for the front of the shortall. Trace the pattern piece onto the fabric. Place the fabric and stabilizer in the embroidery hoop so the embroidery will be stitched where shown on the pattern piece. Embroider the design as desired. Remove the fabric from the hoop and tear off the stabilizer.

2 Cut out the embroidered front.

3 Serge or zigzag stitch the lower edges of the facings. With right sides together, sew the front facing to the front along the armholes, neckline and straps. Clip the curves; trim the seam allowances and turn to the right side. Repeat with the back facing and the back.

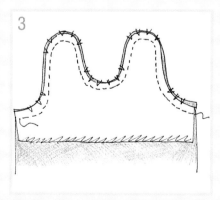

4 Sew the side seams with right sides together. Press open.

5 Press the lower edges of the shortall ¼" to the wrong side. Press again another ½" and stitch.

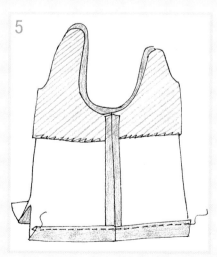

6 Sew the inner leg seam.

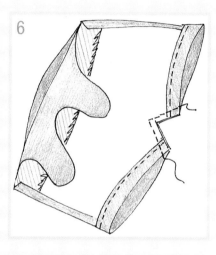

7 Sew the snaps to the ends of the straps as marked on the pattern piece. The front strap should overlap on top of the back strap. Sew the buttons on the front straps over the snaps.

1 Sew the four cap sections together. Press seam allowances to one side.

2 Place the brim interfacing onto the wrong side of one of the brims and baste around the edges. Trim the interfacing along the outside of the stitching. Sew the brims with right sides together along the outer curved edges. Clip the curves; trim the seam and turn to the right side. Press.

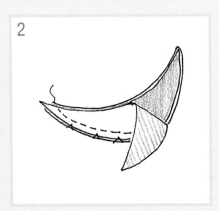

3 Center the brim along one of the cap sections and stitch with right sides together.

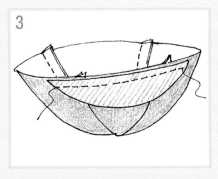

4 Beginning at the back of the cap, open out one side of the bias tape and stitch with right sides together along the lower edge of the cap, turning the beginning end under ¼". When you have stitched all the way around, clip off the excess tape. Press the tape to the inside and stitch close to the other side of the bias tape.

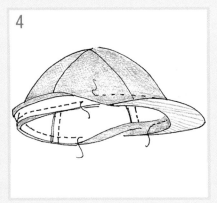

5 If cap does not fit snugly on the head, zigzag stitch a 1½"-2" piece of ⅛" elastic along the inside of the back of the hat (optional).

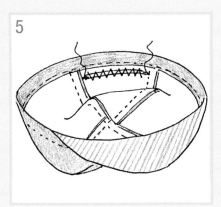

PLEATED DRESS WITH FELT SHOES

SUPPLIES

½ yd. (½ yd., ¾ yd., ¾ yd.) striped or gingham cotton fabric

¼ yd. white cotton fabric for the collar and cuffs

Package of white bias tape

21" white ribbon for ribbon flowers, ⅛" wide

3 buttons, size ¼", for the flower centers

3" (4", 6", 6") Velcro strip

9" x 12" piece of felt

2 buttons, size ¼" for the shoes

2 small snaps

CUTTING INSTRUCTIONS

From the striped or gingham cotton fabric, cut:
• One dress front (Pattern 19).
• Two dress backs (Pattern 20).
• Two dress sleeves (Pattern 8).

From the white cotton fabric, cut:
• Four dress collars (Pattern 18).
• Two 1½" x 5" (5", 6½", 7") cuffs.

From the felt, cut:
• Two shoe uppers (Pattern 24).
• Two shoe straps (Pattern 22).
• Two shoe soles (Pattern 23).

Note: If you want the inside edge and the strap of the shoes to have a pinked edge, cut along these cutting lines with a pinking shears.

PLEATED DRESS

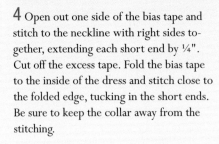

1 To make the three box pleats in the front, begin with the center pleat. Make the center pleat by folding the sides of the pleat to the center front and pin. Sew the pleat from the neckline to the dot marked on the pattern piece. Make the two side pleats in the same manner. Press the pleats flat.

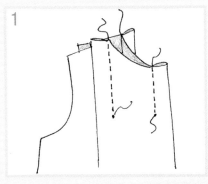

2 With right sides together, sew the shoulder seams and press the seam allowances open. Press the center back edges ¼" to the wrong side and stitch.

3 With two collars right sides together, sew the outer seam. Repeat with the remaining two collars. Clip the curves; turn to the right side and press. Place the collars on the center front of the neckline and baste. *Note:* The collars don't extend all the way to the center back edges.

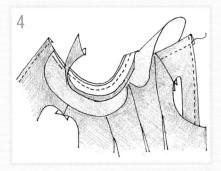

4 Open out one side of the bias tape and stitch to the neckline with right sides together, extending each short end by ¼". Cut off the excess tape. Fold the bias tape to the inside of the dress and stitch close to the folded edge, tucking in the short ends. Be sure to keep the collar away from the stitching.

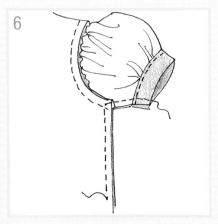

5 Gather the lower edge of each sleeve to fit the cuffs. Press one long edge of each cuff ¼" to the wrong side. With the right side of the unpressed edge of the cuff to the wrong side of the sleeve, sew each cuff to the lower edges of the sleeves. Fold each cuff to the right side and stitch close to the folded edge.

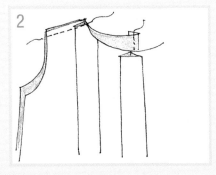

6 Gather the sleeve caps between dots marked on the pattern piece. Sew the sleeve caps to the armholes with right sides together. Sew the underarm seams from the cuffs to the hem of the dress.

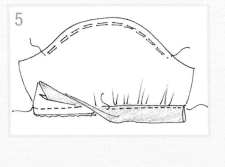

7 Serge or zigzag stitch the hem of the dress. Press this edge ¼" to the wrong side and stitch.

8 For the flowers, cut the ribbon in three equal pieces. Make five ½" loops with each piece and tack to the bottom of the stitching of each front pleat. Sew a button to the center of each flower.

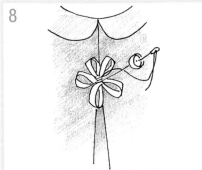

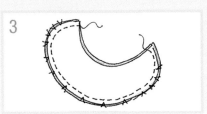

9 Lapping right over left, sew the Velcro to the back opening.

1 With right sides together, sew the heel seam of the uppers. Carefully pin the sole to the upper with right sides together. Stitch. Turn to the right side.

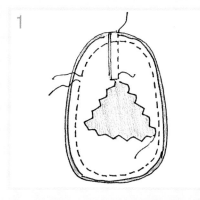

2 Sew one half of a snap to the shoe as marked on the pattern piece. Sew the other half to the underside of the end of the straps. Sew a button over the snap on the right side of the strap.

3 Stitch the straight end of the strap to the inside of the shoe as marked on the pattern piece.

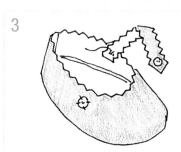

BITTY TWINS (BOY) BY PLEASANT COMPANY AND GÖTZ

The same outfits can be made from matching blue gingham fabric for a classic look.

Under Construction

CITITOY

Coverall outfits are perfect for playtime in the sandbox. The coveralls are merely longer versions of the shortalls. The boy's version features cotton fabric with a colorful car and truck print. The theme is carried out in the car embroidery on the pocket. The coveralls are paired with a lime green long-sleeved T-shirt and a ball cap. The girl's bright pink coveralls are cut from the same pattern pieces, but have an elastic casing at the ankles. The dainty floral embroidery is stitched directly on the front. She wears a polka-dot long-sleeved blouse under her coveralls. Her hat is the same shape, but with a polka-dot ruffle sewn along the edge.

LONG-SLEEVED T-SHIRT, COVERALLS AND CAP

SUPPLIES

¼ yd. green knit fabric

1½" x 13½" (15", 16½", 17") green ribbing

½ yd. (½ yd., ⅔ yd., ¾ yd.) print cotton fabric for the coveralls and cap

2" (3", 4", 4") Velcro strip

2 small snaps

2 buttons, size ¼" (¼", ½", ½")

Scrap of green woven fabric for the pocket

Car embroidery design*

40 wt. embroidery thread

Tear-away stabilizer

Scrap of medium weight interfacing for the cap

Package of bias tape to match the color of hat

1½"-2" elastic, ⅛" wide (optional)

*Used in this project: "Young At Heart 1" by Cactus Punch

CUTTING INSTRUCTIONS

From the green knit fabric, cut:
• One shirt front (Pattern 9).
• Two shirt backs (Pattern 10).
• Two shirt sleeves (Pattern 25).

From the green ribbing, cut:
• One 1½" x 6½" (7½", 9", 9½") strip for the neckline.
• Cut the remaining ribbing in half widthwise for the cuffs.

From the print cotton fabric, cut:
• One coverall front (Pattern 11).
• One coverall front facing (Pattern 11).
• One coverall back (Pattern 12).
• One coverall back facing (Pattern 12).
• Four cap sections (Pattern 14).
• Two cap brims (Pattern 15).

From the interfacing, cut:
• One cap brim (Pattern 15).

From the scrap of green woven fabric:
• Note: Leave room for two pockets (Pattern 13).
  See Steps 1-2.

LONG-SLEEVED T-SHIRT

1 Press the center back edges ¼" to the wrong side and stitch. With right sides together, sew the shoulder seams with a serger or zigzag stitch.

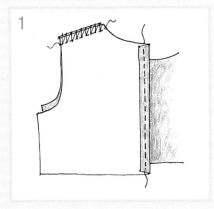

2 Fold the neckline ribbing in half lengthwise with right sides together. Stitch the short ends and turn to the right side. Stretching the ribbing to fit the neckline, serge or zigzag stitch the ribbing to the neckline.

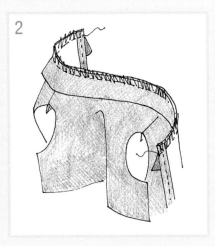

3 Fold the cuff ribbing in half lengthwise with wrong sides together. Sew the cuff to the bottom of the sleeve with right sides together, stretching to fit. Repeat with the other sleeve and cuff.

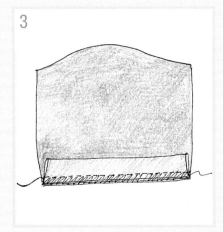

4 With right sides together, serge or zigzag stitch the sleeves to the shirt armholes, easing as necessary.

5 Serge or zigzag stitch the underarm seam, starting at the sleeve hem and finishing at the lower edge of the shirt.

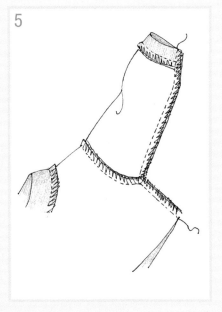

6 Serge or zigzag stitch the lower edge of the shirt. Press the edge ⅜" to the wrong side and topstitch.

7 Lapping right over left, sew the Velcro to the back opening.

1 For the pocket, cut a piece of green woven fabric to fit in your machine's embroidery hoop. Hoop with stabilizer and stitch the embroidery design. Tear away the stabilizer and cut the pocket using the pattern piece with the embroidery in the center.

2 Cut a second pocket the same size from the remaining scrap piece. With right sides together, sew around all sides of the pocket, leaving an opening on one of the sides. Clip the corners; turn to the right side and press.

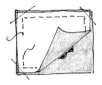

3 Sew the pocket on the front as marked on the pattern piece on the sides and bottom edges to the front of the coveralls.

4 Serge or zigzag stitch the lower edges of the facings. With the right sides together, sew the front facing to the front along the armholes, neckline and straps. Clip the curves; trim the seam allowances and turn to the right side. Repeat with the back facing and the back.

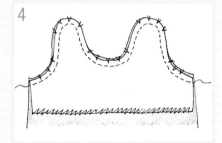

5 Sew the side seams with right sides together. Press open.

6 Press the lower edges of the coveralls ¼" to the wrong side. Press again another ½" and stitch.

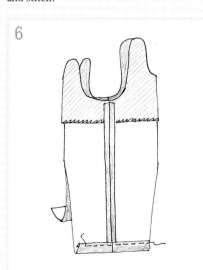

7 Sew the inner leg seam.

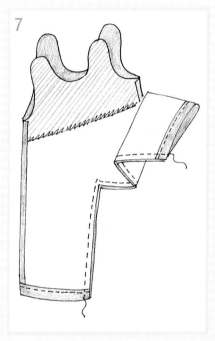

8 Sew the snaps to the ends of the straps as marked on the pattern piece. The front strap should overlap on top of the back strap. Sew the buttons on the front straps over the snaps.

CAP

1 Sew the four cap sections together. Press the seam allowances to one side.

3 Center the brim along one of the cap sections and stitch with right sides together.

5 If the cap does not fit snugly on the head, zigzag stitch a 1½"-2" piece of ⅛" elastic along the inside of the back of the hat.

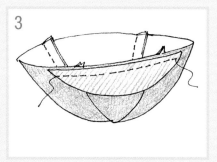

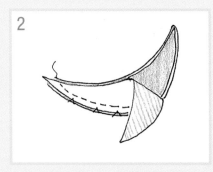

2 Place the brim interfacing on the wrong side of one of the brims and baste around the edges. Trim the interfacing along the outside of the stitching. Sew the brims with right sides together along the outer curved edges. Clip the curves; trim the seam and turn to the right side. Press.

4 Beginning at the back of the cap, open out one side of the bias tape and stitch with right sides together along the lower edge of the cap, turning the beginning end under ¼". When you have stitched all the way around, clip off the excess tape. Press the tape to the inside and stitch close to the other side of the bias tape.

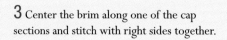

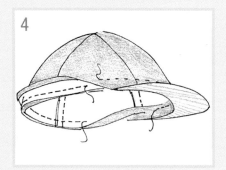

BLOUSE, GIRL'S COVERALLS AND RUFFLED HAT

SUPPLIES

¼ yd. polka dot cotton fabric

6½" (7", 8", 8") elastic for the sleeves, ⅛" wide

2" (3", 4", 4") Velcro strip

½ yd. (½ yd., ⅔ yd., ¾ yd.) pink cotton fabric for the coveralls and hat

6½" (9", 9½", 10") elastic for the pant legs, ⅛" wide

Package of bias tape to match the coverall fabric

2 small snaps

2 buttons, size ¼" (¼", ½", ½")

Floral embroidery design*

40 wt. embroidery thread

Tear-away stabilizer

*Used in this project: "Little Bits 2" by Cactus Punch

CUTTING INSTRUCTIONS

From the polka dot cotton fabric, cut:
- Two blouse fronts (Pattern 9).
- Four blouse backs (Pattern 10).
- Two blouse sleeves (Pattern 8).
- Four blouse collars (Pattern 18).
- One 3" x 17" (3" x 21", 4" x 24", 4" x 24") ruffle.

From the pink cotton fabric, cut:
- One coverall front facing (Pattern 11).
- One coverall back (Pattern 12).
- One coverall back facing (Pattern 12).
- Four hat sections (Pattern 14).
- *Note:* Leave enough fabric to fit under the embroidery hoop for the coverall front (Pattern 11).

BLOUSE

1 With the right sides together, sew a front to two backs at the shoulders. Press the seam allowances open. Repeat with the remaining pieces for the lining.

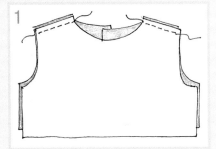

2 Place two collar pieces right sides together and stitch around the outside edge. Trim the seam allowance; clip the curves and turn to the right side. Press. Repeat with the other collar pieces.

3 Pin the collars to the neckline of the blouse so they meet at the center front. Baste. *Note:* The collars don't extend all the way to the center back edges.

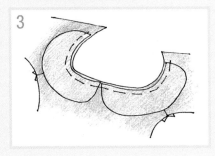

4 With right sides together, sew the lining to the blouse along one center back, around the neckline, down the other center back, sandwiching the collar in between. Stitch along both lower edges in back and the lower edge in the front. Clip the curves and turn to the right side. Press. Baste the armholes together.

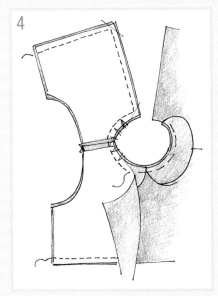

5 Narrow-hem the bottom of each sleeve edge. Cut the sleeve elastic in half. Starting at one side of the sleeve and ½" from the hemmed edge, sew the elastic by zigzag stitching over the top, stretching the elastic to the other side of the sleeve. Do not catch the elastic in your stitching except to secure the ends at each side.

6 Gather the sleeve caps between the dots marked on the pattern piece.

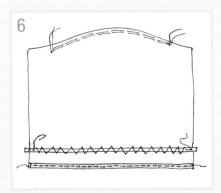

7 With right sides together, sew the sleeve caps to the armholes. Sew the underarm seam.

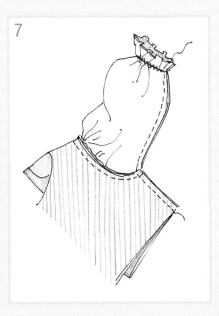

GIRL'S COVERALLS

1 To embroider the front of the coveralls, cut a piece of pink fabric big enough for the front of the coveralls. Trace the pattern piece onto the fabric. Place the fabric and stabilizer in the embroidery hoop so the embroidery will be stitched where shown on the pattern piece. Embroider the design as desired. Remove from hoop and tear off the stabilizer.

2 Cut out the embroidered front.

3 Serge or zigzag stitch the lower edges of the facings. With the right sides together, sew the front facing to the front along the armholes, neckline and straps. Clip the curves; trim the seam allowances and turn to the right side. Repeat with the back facing and the back.

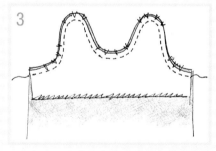

4 Sew the side seams with right sides together. Press open.

5 Cut a piece of bias tape to fit the bottom of one of the pant legs. Open out one of the sides of the bias tape and stitch to the bottom of the pant legs with right sides together. Press the tape to the inside of the leg and stitch close to the folded edge of the tape to make a casing. Cut the pant leg elastic in half and thread one of the pieces through the casing and secure at each end. Repeat with the other pant leg.

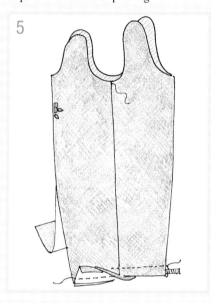

6 Sew the inner leg seam with right sides together.

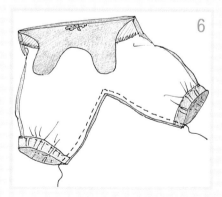

7 Sew the snaps to the ends of the straps as marked on the pattern piece. The front strap should overlap on top of the back strap. Sew the buttons on the front straps over the snaps.

RUFFLED HAT

1 Sew all the hat sections together. Press the seam allowances to one side.

2 Sew the short ends of the ruffle with right sides together. Turn to the right side and fold the ruffle in half lengthwise. Press.

3 Gather the raw edges of the ruffle to fit the bottom of the hat.

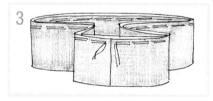

4 Stitch the ruffle to the hat with right sides together.

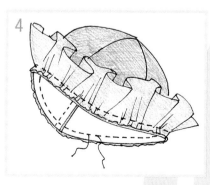

5 Serge or zigzag stitch the seam to finish the raw edge.

Bonjour Velour

COROLLE

Soft, cuddly velour or other brushed fabrics are wonderful for baby doll clothing. This outfit features a top with a Peter Pan collar, heart-shaped pockets and a ruffled hem. The pants are made from a complementary print velour fabric. The beret has a wide band with a print velour fabric bow at the front. When working with napped fabrics, always press from the wrong side to avoid flattening the nap with the iron.

TOP WITH RUFFLED HEM, BERET AND PANTS

SUPPLIES

½ yd. (⅔ yd., ⅔ yd., ⅔ yd.) solid color velour or other knit fabric

⅓ yd. (⅓ yd., ½ yd., ½ yd.) print velour or other knit fabric

Scrap of woven fabric for the pocket lining

2 buttons, size ¼" (⅜", ⅜", ⅜")

⅓ yd. satin ribbon, ¼" wide

2" (3", 4", 4") Velcro strip

8" (11", 14", 17") elastic, ⅜" wide

Package of single fold bias tape to match the solid color fabric

Temporary spray adhesive

CUTTING INSTRUCTIONS

From the solid fabric, cut:
- One top front (Pattern 9).
- Two top backs (Pattern 10).
- Two top sleeves (Pattern 25).
- Four top collars (Pattern 18).
- One 1¾" x 26" (1¾" x 32", 2" x 44", 2½" x 44") ruffle.
- One 11½" (11½", 13", 13") diameter circle for the beret top.
- One 2" x 11" (2" x 13½", 2½" x 14", 2½" x 15½") band for the beret.

From the print fabric, cut:
- Four pants (Pattern 26).
- One bow (Pattern 27).
- One bow center (Pattern 28).
- *Note:* Leave room for two pockets (Pattern 77). See Step 5.

1 With right sides together, sew the backs to the front at the shoulders. Press the seam allowances open. Press the center back edges ½" to the wrong side and stitch.

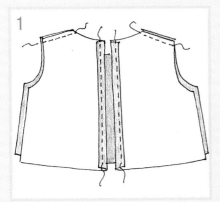

2 Pin two collars with right sides together. Stitch along the curved outside edge. Clip the curves; trim the seam and turn to the right side. Press. Repeat with the remaining collars.

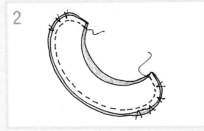

3 Pin the collars to the neckline so that they meet at the center front. Baste. *Note:* They will not extend all the way to the back edges.

4 Unfold one side of the bias tape and pin it to the neckline with right sides together, extending the short ends by ¼". Cut off the excess. Stitch to the neckline. Fold the bias tape over to the inside of the top and stitch close to the other folded side, tucking in the short ends. Be sure to keep the collars away from your stitching.

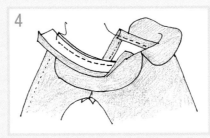

5 For the pockets, trace two pocket shapes on one side of the lining fabric. Spray the other side of the lining with temporary spray adhesive (this is used to keep the velour fabric from shifting while stitching). Place the right side of print velour fabric on top of the sprayed side of the lining. Turn it over and stitch all the way around the pocket shapes, following the ¼" seam allowance. Cut along the outside edges and clip the curves. Slash the lining fabric only and turn the pocket to the right side (the adhesive will disappear). Stitch to the front of the top as marked on the pattern piece, stitching between the dots marked on the pocket pattern piece.

6 Press the lower edges of the sleeves ¼" to the wrong side and stitch. With right sides together, sew the sleeve caps to the armholes, easing as necessary. Sew the underarm seams from the sleeve edge to the lower edge of the top.

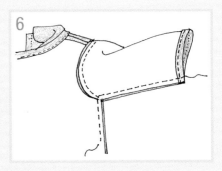

7 Narrow-hem one long edge and both short ends of the ruffle. Gather the top edge of the ruffle to fit the lower edge of the top and stitch with right sides together.

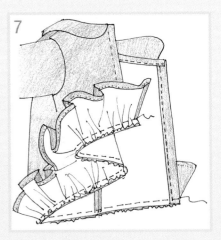

8 Sew the buttons to the top as marked on the pattern piece. Tie a bow with the satin ribbon and tack between the collars in the front.

9 Lapping right over left, sew the Velcro to the back opening.

BERET

1 Gather the outside edge of the beret top.

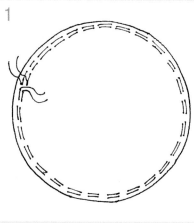

2 With right sides together, sew the short ends of the band. Fold the band in half lengthwise with wrong sides together. Sew the top to the band with right sides together and finish the seams.

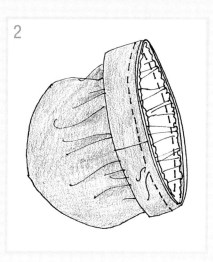

3 Fold the bow in half lengthwise with right sides together. Stitch along one end and the long edges. Turn to the right side.

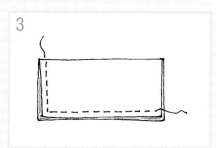

4 Fold the remaining edges of the short end to the inside and slip stitch closed. Press the long sides of the bow center ¼" to the wrong side. Wrap around the bow, pinching tightly so the ends meet at the back of the bow and hand stitch in place.

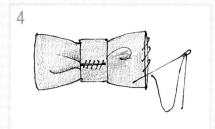

PANTS

1 With right sides together, sew the pant side seams and the center front and back seams.

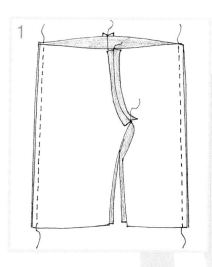

2 Press the lower edge of the pants ¼" to the wrong side and stitch.

3 Serge or zigzag stitch the top edge of the pants. Press the top edge of the pants ¾" to the wrong side. Stitch ½" from the folded edge, leaving a 1" opening in the back. Thread the elastic through the casing and secure the ends. Stitch the opening closed.

4 Sew the inner leg seam.

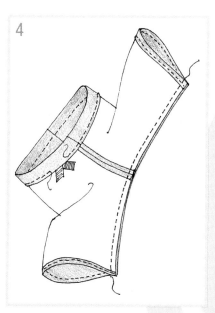

Denim Play Date

BITTY TWINS BY PLEASANT COMPANY

Denim is a very versatile fabric for playtime doll clothes. It is a wardrobe staple and coordinates well with many different colors. Just be sure to use a lightweight denim or chambray when working with such small garments. It can be decorated in many ways, such as appliqué and machine embroidery. The boy's pants have a machine embroidered train on the bib front and red cuffs on the pant legs. The girl's jumper has a bouquet of flowers made from felt. They are stitched with green thread to make the stems. Both boy and girl outfits coordinate well with knit shirts.

SHORT-SLEEVED T-SHIRT AND DENIM PANTS WITH BIB

SUPPLIES

¼ yd. striped knit fabric

1½" x 6½" (7½", 9", 9½") white ribbing

2" (3", 4", 4") Velcro strip for the shirt

⅓ yd. (½ yd., ½ yd., ½ yd.) lightweight denim fabric

Package of piping in contrasting color

1¾" x 13" (2" x 17", 2" x 19", 2" x 19") piece of red cotton fabric for the cuffs

2 buttons, size ⅜" (⅜", ½", ½")

4½" (5", 7½", 7½") elastic, ¼" wide

2 Velcro strips, each ½" long for the straps on the pants

Train machine embroidery design*

40 wt. embroidery thread

Self-adhesive tear-away stabilizer

*Used in this project: "Me and My Doll Clothes" by Joan Hinds for VSM Sewing, Inc.

CUTTING INSTRUCTIONS

From the striped knit fabric, cut:
- •One T-shirt front (Pattern 9).
- •Two T-shirt backs (Pattern 10).
- •Two T-shirt sleeves (Pattern 25).

From the denim, cut:
- •One pant front (Pattern 29).
- •One pant front facing (Pattern 33).
- •One pant back (Pattern 30).
- •Two 1¾" x 7" (2" x 8", 2" x 9½", 2" x 9½") straps.

T-SHIRT

1 Press the center back edges ¼" to the wrong side and stitch.

2 With right sides together, sew the shoulder seams with a serger or zigzag stitch. Fold the ribbing in half lengthwise with right sides together. Stitch the short ends and turn to the right side. Stretching the ribbing to fit the neckline, serge or zigzag stitch the ribbing to the neckline.

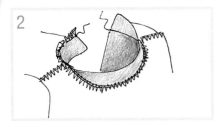

3 Serge or zigzag stitch the lower edges of the sleeves. Press ¼" to the wrong side and topstitch. With right sides together, serge or zigzag stitch the sleeves to the shirt armholes, easing as necessary.

4 Serge or zigzag stitch the underarm seam, starting at the sleeve hem and finishing at the lower edge of the shirt.

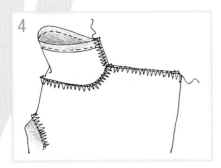

5 Serge or zigzag stitch the lower edge of the shirt, press the edge ⅜" to the wrong side and topstitch.

6 Lapping right over left, sew the Velcro to the back opening.

DENIM PANTS WITH BIB

1 Place sticky stabilizer in the machine embroidery hoop and place the front overall over the stabilizer. The fabric does not need to be hooped, but should be secure on the stabilizer (or follow your machine's embroidery instructions). The design should be centered over the area marked on the pattern piece. Embroider the design and remove stabilizer from the back.

2 Pin the piping to the curved top edge of the overalls and baste. Serge or zigzag stitch the lower straight edge of the facing. With right sides together, stitch the facing to the piped edge of the overalls. Clip the curves, turn to the right side and press.

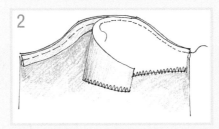

3 Press the top edge of the back ¼" to the wrong side. Press again another ½" and stitch to form the casing. Thread the elastic through the casing and secure at each end.

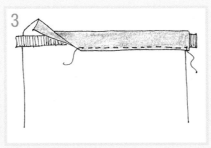

4 With right sides together, sew the side seams.

5 Cut the red strip in half widthwise. Fold each strip in half lengthwise with wrong sides together and press to form a cuff. Stitch the right side of the cuff to the wrong side of each pant leg. Fold the cuff over to the right side and press.

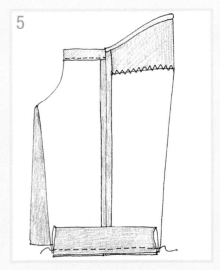

6 Stitch the inner leg seam.

7 Press the long edges of the each strap ¼" to the wrong side. Press one end of each strap ¼" to the wrong side. Fold the straps in half lengthwise and press. Stitch the straps together along the folded edges and the short end. Stitch the loop side of the Velcro to the stitched end of the strap.

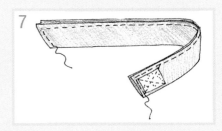

8 Stitch each strap to the wrong side of the back waist approximately 1" from the center. Sew the hook side of the Velcro to the wrong side of the front overalls as marked on the pattern piece. Sew a button to the right side of the front over the Velcro stitching.

KNIT SHIRT AND DENIM JUMPER

SUPPLIES

¼ yd. print knit fabric

8" (8", 11", 11") elastic for the sleeves, ⅛" wide

2" (3", 4", 4") Velcro strip

Package of single fold bias tape to match shirt fabric

¼ yd. (⅓ yd., ½ yd., ½ yd.) lightweight denim

Package of piping in contrasting color

4½" (5", 7½", 7½") elastic, ¼" wide

Scraps of yellow and red felt

Green machine embroidery thread

¼ yd. red ribbon, ⅛" wide

CUTTING INSTRUCTIONS

From the print knit fabric, cut:
- One shirt front (Pattern 9).
- Two shirt backs (Pattern 10).
- Two shirt sleeves (Pattern 8).
- Four shirt collars (Pattern 18).

From the lightweight denim, cut:
- One jumper front (Pattern 31).
- One jumper front facing (Pattern 33).
- One jumper back (Pattern 32).
- Four pockets (Pattern 34).
- Two 1¾" x 7" (2" x 8", 2" x 9½", 2" x 9½") straps.
- Two 1" x 4" (1" x 4", 1½" x 5", 1½" x 5") pocket ruffles.

From the red felt, cut:
- Two flowers (Pattern 35).
- One flower center (Pattern 36).

From the yellow felt, cut:
- One flower (Pattern 35).
- Two flower centers (Pattern 36).

KNIT SHIRT

1 Press the center back edges ¼" to the wrong side and stitch.

2 With right sides together, sew the shoulder seams with a serger or zigzag stitch.

3 With right sides together, sew two collar pieces together along the curved outside edge. Clip the curves, turn to the right side and press. Topstitch close to the pressed edge. Repeat with the remaining two collar pieces.

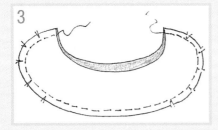

4 Place the collars along the neckline edge; baste. *Note:* The collars will meet at the center front, but will not extend all the way to the center back opening.

5 Open out the bias tape and stitch it to the neck edge with right sides together, extending the ends of the tape ¼" beyond the center backs. Cut off the excess.

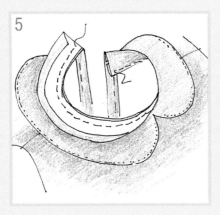

6 Turn the tape to the inside of the shirt and stitch along the remaining edge, tucking in the short ends. Be sure to keep the collars away from your stitching.

7 Serge or zigzag the lower edge of each sleeve and press ¼" to the wrong side. Stitch.

8 Cut the sleeve elastic in half. Starting at one side of the sleeve and ½" from the hemmed edge, sew the sleeve elastic by zigzag stitching over the top, stretching the elastic to the other side of the sleeve. Do not catch the elastic in your stitching except to secure the ends at each side.

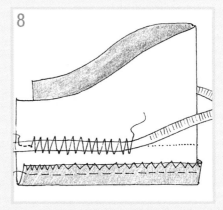

9 Gather the top edge of the sleeves between the dots. With right sides together, stitch each sleeve to the armhole of the shirt.

10 Sew the underarm seam.

11 Serge or zigzag stitch the bottom of the shirt, press the edge ⅜" to the wrong side and stitch.

12 Lapping right over left, sew the Velcro to the back opening.

1 Pin the piping to the curved top edge of the jumper and baste. Serge or zigzag stitch the lower straight edge of the facing. With right sides together, stitch the facing to the piped edge of the jumper. Clip the curves, turn to the right side and press.

2 Stitch a length of piping across the top edge of each pocket. Sew to another pocket with right sides together around all edges, leaving a small opening for turning. Clip the curves and turn to the right side. Press. Repeat for the remaining two pockets.

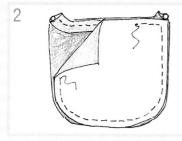

3 Press one long side and both short ends of a pocket ruffle ¼" to the wrong side and stitch. Gather the other long edge and stitch this edge to the underside of the pocket along the piped seam edge.

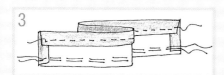

4 Place the pockets on the jumper where marked on the pattern piece. Stitch closely along the curved outside edge.

5 To decorate the jumper, place the red and yellow felt flowers on the jumper front, as marked on the pattern piece. Following the lines on the pattern piece and using green thread, stitch the lines for stems using a reinforced straight stitch or by hand (you will be stitching through the flowers). Tie a bow and glue to the stems where they meet. Glue the centers to each flower, using a contrasting color center for each.

6 Press the top edge of the back ¼" to the wrong side. Press again another ½" and stitch to form the casing. Thread the elastic through the casing and secure at each end.

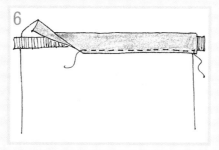

7 With right sides together, sew the side seams. Serge or zigzag stitch the lower edge of the skirt. Press this edge ⅜" to the wrong side and topstitch.

8 Press the long edges of each strap ¼" to the wrong side. Press one end of each strap ¼" to the wrong side. Fold the strips in half lengthwise and press. Stitch the straps together along the folded edges and the short end. Stitch the loop side of the Velcro to the stitched end of the strap.

9 Stitch each strap to the wrong side of the back waist approximately 1" from the center.

10 Sew the hook side of the Velcro to the wrong side of the front overalls as marked on the pattern piece.

11 Sew a button to the right side of the front over the Velcro stitching.

Trick-or-Treat

ZAPF CREATION

This doll is ready for trick-or-treating in his outfit. The sweat suit is a basic jacket with ribbing at the neck and cuffs, elastic waist pants with ribbing at the ankles, and a cap with ribbing for the band along the edge. It becomes a pumpkin when orange stretch terry fabric is used with bright green ribbing. The face on the pocket is cut out of black felt. To complete the outfit, add a curled chenille stem and green felt leaf to the hat.

JACKET, PANTS AND CAP

SUPPLIES

⅓ yd. (½ yd., ½ yd., ⅔ yd.) orange stretch terry fabric

Scrap of orange woven fabric for the pocket lining

⅛ yd. green ribbing

Scrap of black felt

Scrap of green felt

Fabric glue

8" (11", 14", 17") elastic, ⅜" wide

3½" (4", 5½", 6½") Velcro strip

3 (3, 5, 5) green buttons, size (¼", ½", ½", ½")

1½" (2", 2", 2") length of a green chenille stem

CUTTING INSTRUCTIONS

From the orange stretch terry fabric, cut:
• Two jacket fronts (Pattern 37).
• One jacket back (Pattern 38).
• Two jacket sleeves (Pattern 25).
• One jacket pocket (Pattern 39).
• Four pants (Pattern 26).
• Four cap sections (Pattern 14).

From the scrap of orange woven fabric, cut:
• One jacket pocket (Pattern 39).

From the green ribbing, cut:
• One 1½" x 7" (7", 9½", 11") strip for the jacket collar.
• Two 1½" x 3" (3½", 4½", 4½") strips for the jacket sleeve cuffs.
• Two 1½" x 4" (1½" x 4", 2" x 5½", 2" x 5½") strips for the pants cuffs.
• One 1½" x 11" (2" x 14", 2" x 14½", 2½" x 17") strip for the cap.

From the scrap of black felt, cut:
• One pumpkin face, following the pattern drawn on the pocket pattern.

From the scrap of green felt, cut:
• One leaf (Pattern 40).

JACKET

1 With right sides together, sew the fronts to the back at the shoulders. Press the seam allowances open. Zigzag stitch or serge the center front edges.

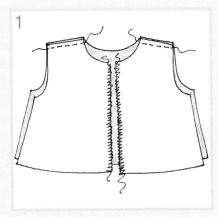

2 To make the pocket, pin the stretch terry and woven fabric pockets right sides together. Stitch around the pocket leaving a 1" opening at the bottom edge of the pocket. Clip the curves; turn to the right side and press.

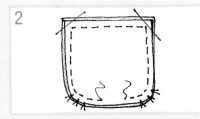

3 Glue the black felt pumpkin face to the pocket with fabric glue, as shown on the pattern piece.

4 Stitch the pocket to the right front jacket as marked on the pattern piece.

5 Fold the ribbing strip for the jacket collar in half lengthwise with wrong sides together. Pin the folded collar around the neckline of the jacket between the center front fold lines, with right sides together. The collar should taper with the cut ends of the collar included in the seam allowance (see illustration below).

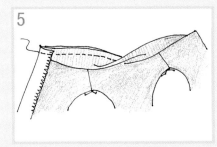

6 Fold the center fronts over the collar along the fold lines with right sides together and pin at the neckline edge. Stitch the collar to the neckline. Turn the center front edges toward the inside of the garment along the fold line indicated on the pattern piece. Press.

7 Fold the ribbing strips for the jacket sleeve cuffs in half lengthwise with wrong sides together to form cuffs. Stretch the cuffs to fit the lower edge of each sleeve and zigzag stitch or serge them together.

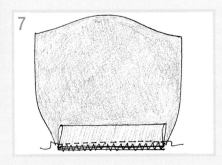

8 Easing as necessary, stitch the sleeves to the armholes with right sides together.

9 Sew the underarm seam from the wrist to the lower edge with right sides together.

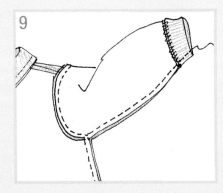

10 Zigzag stitch or serge the hem of the jacket. Press this edge ½" to the wrong side and stitch ⅜" from the pressed edge.

11 Lapping right over left, sew the Velcro to the front opening.

12 Sew the green buttons to the top of the right front jacket, spacing them equally.

PANTS

CAP

1 With right sides together, sew the center front and center back seams.

2 Sew the side seams with right sides together.

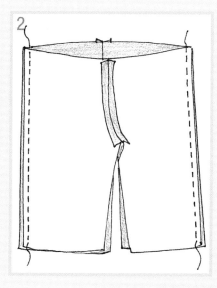

3 Fold each ribbing strip for the pant cuffs in half lengthwise with wrong sides together and stitch to the bottom of each pant leg, stretching to fit.

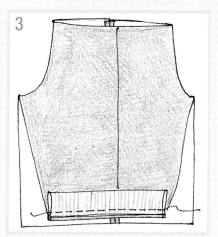

4 Sew the inner leg seam.

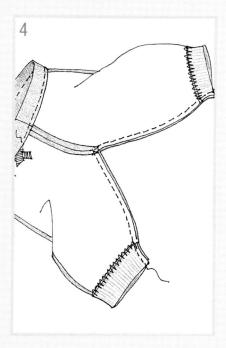

5 Serge or zigzag stitch the top of the pants and press ¾" to the wrong side. Stitch ½" from the pressed edge, leaving a 1" opening at the back. Thread the elastic in the casing and secure the ends. Stitch the opening closed.

1 With right sides together, sew all the sections together.

2 With right sides together, sew the short ends of the ribbing strip for the cap together. Fold the ribbing in half lengthwise with the wrong sides together. Sew the ribbing to the cap edge with right sides together.

3 Coil the chenille stem around a pencil a couple of times to resemble a curled pumpkin stem. Make a small cut in the seam line on top of the hat and insert the stem. Tack the stem to the hat with a few hand stitches.

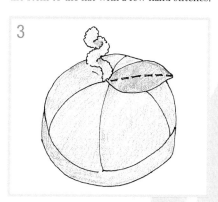

4 Make a line of stitches by hand with a double length of green thread down the middle of the leaf. Tack one end to the base of the stem on the cap.

Winter Wonderland

BITTY BABY BY PLEASANT COMPANY

When this doll saw all the fun her friend in the Pumpkin Sweat Suit was having, she wanted to get in on the act as well! This sweat suit can be modified for three different seasons and made from three different fabrics. It truly is an easy and very versatile garment. The Winter Sweat Suit is sewn from sweatshirt fleece with snowflake buttons on the front. It has a long stocking cap, which is helpful when the cold winds blow.

JACKET, PANTS AND HAT

Make a new sweat suit for each season. Here, the Patriotic Sweat Suit is sewn from woven stars and stripes fabric with red, white and blue star buttons. The Valentine Sweat Suit is made from polar fleece, heart buttons and heart shaped pockets. The pockets are not lined, but sewn closely along the cut edges to the jacket.

GÖTZ

BERENGUER

SUPPLIES

⅓ yd. (½ yd., ½ yd., ⅔ yd.) blue sweatshirt fleece

Scrap of blue woven fabric for the pocket lining

⅛ yd. white ribbing

8" (11", 14", 17") elastic, ⅜" wide

3½" (4", 5½", 6½") Velcro strip

3 (3, 5, 5) novelty snowflake buttons

White pompom, 1"

10½" (12", 13", 14½") elastic for the hat, ¼" wide

Package of white bias tape

CUTTING INSTRUCTIONS

From the sweatshirt fleece, cut:
•Two jacket fronts (Pattern 37).
•One jacket back (Pattern 38).
•Two jacket sleeves (Pattern 25).
•One jacket pocket (Pattern 39).
•Four pants (Pattern 26).
•Two hat pieces (Pattern 42).

From the blue woven fabric, cut:
•One jacket pocket (Pattern 39).

From the white ribbing, cut:
•One 1½" x 7" (7", 9½", 11") strip for the collar.
•Two 1½" x 3" (3½", 4½", 4½") strips for the sleeve cuffs.
•Two 1½" x 4" (1½" x 4", 2" x 5½", 2" x 5½") strips for the pant cuffs.

JACKET

JACKET

1 With right sides together, sew the fronts to the back at the shoulders. Press the seam allowances open.

2 Zigzag stitch or serge the center front edges.

3 To make the pocket, pin the sweatshirt fleece and woven fabric pocket right sides together. Stitch around the pocket leaving a 1" opening at the bottom edge of the pocket. Clip the curves and turn to the right side. Press. Stitch the pocket to the right front jacket as marked on the pattern piece.

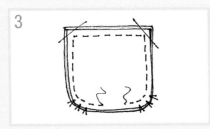

4 Fold the ribbing strip for the collar in half lengthwise with wrong sides together. Pin the folded collar around the neckline of the jacket between the center front fold lines with right sides together. The collar should taper with the cut ends of the collar included in the seam allowance (see illustration below).

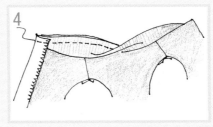

5 Fold the center fronts over the collar along the fold lines with right sides together and pin at the neckline edge. Stitch the collar to the neckline. Turn the center front edges toward the inside of the garment along the fold line indicated on the pattern piece. Press.

6 Fold the ribbing strip for the cuff in half lengthwise with wrong sides together. Stretch the cuffs to fit the lower edge of each sleeve and zigzag stitch or serge.

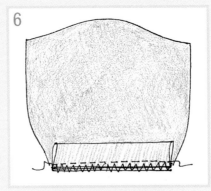

7 Easing as necessary, stitch the sleeves to the armholes with right sides together.

8 Sew the underarm seam from the wrist to the lower edge with right sides together.

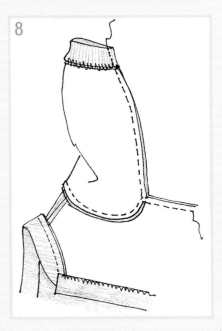

9 Zigzag stitch or serge the hem of the jacket. Press this edge ½" to the wrong side and stitch ⅜" from the pressed edge.

10 Sew the Velcro to the front opening of the jacket.

11 Sew the snowflake buttons to the top of the jacket front, spacing them equally.

PANTS

HAT

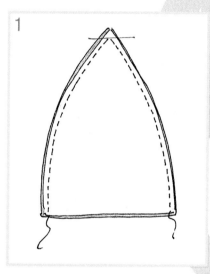

1 If you are using heavier fabrics, such as sweatshirt fleece, cut off ¾" (1", 1", 1") from the bottom of each pant leg to eliminate bulk.

2 With right sides together, sew the center front and center back seams.

3 Sew the side seams with right sides together.

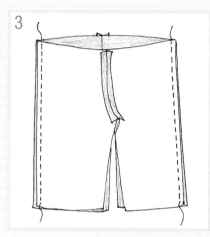

4 Fold each ribbing strip for the pant cuff in half lengthwise with wrong sides together and stitch to the bottom of each pant leg, stretching to fit.

5 Sew the inner leg seam.

6 Serge or zigzag stitch the top of the pants and press ¾" to the wrong side. Stitch ½" from the pressed edge, leaving a 1" opening at the back. Thread the elastic in the casing and secure the ends. Stitch the opening closed.

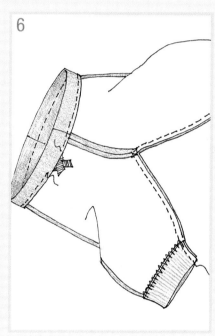

1 With right sides together, sew the hat pieces along the side edges.

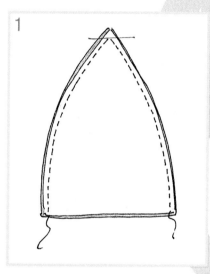

2 Cut a piece of bias tape to fit the lower edge of the hat plus ½". Open out one side of the bias tape and with right sides together, stitch it to the lower edge of the hat, overlapping the ends. Fold the tape over to the wrong side of the hat and stitch, leaving a 1" opening. Insert the elastic in the casing and secure the ends. Stitch the opening closed.

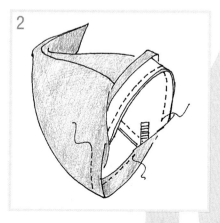

3 Stitch the pompom to the end of the hat.

Gone Fishin'

ADORA DOLLS

When dolls want to go fishing, they need proper attire for playtime outdoors. The bib overalls and jumper are just the right outfits. The boy's overalls are sewn from a plaid fabric and are worn with a frog print woven cotton shirt. The frog motif is carried through onto the embroidered motif on the pocket. He also wears a ball cap made from matching fabric. The girl's overall jumper is made from the same frog print with a pink background color instead of blue. Her pocket and hemline are trimmed with baby rickrack. She wears a long-sleeved knit T-shirt with elastic at the wrists. The wide-brimmed hat, sewn from the pink frog print fabric, will help protect against any rainy weather.

BIB OVERALLS, SHIRT AND CAP

SUPPLIES

⅓ yd. (⅓ yd., ½ yd., ½ yd.) woven plaid fabric

¼ yd. (⅓ yd., ⅓ yd., ½ yd.) frog or other print cotton fabric

Set of overall buckles and slides*

Pair of overall buttons*

Scrap of yellow fabric for pocket

Frog embroidery design*

40 wt. embroidery thread

Tear away stabilizer

4½" (5", 7½", 7½") elastic, ⅜" wide

3 (4, 4, 4) buttons, size ¼"

3 (4, 4, 4) small snaps

Scrap of medium-weight interfacing for the cap

Package of bias tape to match the color of the hat

1½"-2" elastic, ⅛" wide (optional)

*Used in this project: Dritz for Dolls, "Doll Clothing Designs" by Joan Hinds for Cactus Punch

CUTTING INSTRUCTIONS

From the woven plaid fabric, cut:
• Two front overall pants (Pattern 46).
• Two back overall pants (Pattern 46).
• Two front bibs (Pattern 48).
• Four cap sections (Pattern 14).
• One 1" x 5¾" (1¼" x 6½", 1¼" x 8½", 1¼" x 9") front band.
• Two 1" x 6¾" (8¾", 9½", 10¼") straps.

From the frog print fabric, cut:
• Four shirt fronts (Pattern 44).
• Two shirt backs (Pattern 45).
• Two shirt sleeves (Pattern 25).
• One shirt collar (Pattern 47).
• Two cap brims (Pattern 15).

From the interfacing, cut:
• One cap brim (Pattern 15).

From the scrap of yellow fabric:
• *Note:* Leave room for two pockets (Pattern 49). See Step 2.

BIB OVERALLS

BIB OVERALLS

1 To embroider on the pocket, hoop the scrap of yellow fabric with stabilizer and stitch the design, making sure to leave enough room for two pocket patterns to be cut out (if your design is too large for the small- and medium-sized pockets, reduce the size of the design by 20 percent with your embroidery software, or omit the embroidery altogether). Remove the scrap from the hoop.

2 Trace the pocket pattern (Pattern 49) on the yellow fabric, centering the design. Cut out the pocket. Cut another pocket from the yellow fabric. With right sides together, sew the pockets together, leaving a small opening. Clip the corners; turn to the right side and press.

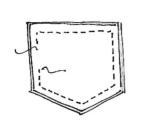

3 With right sides together, sew the center front and back seams of the pants.

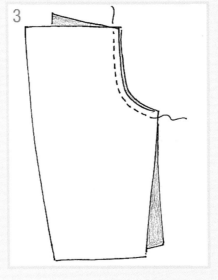

4 Gather the top edge of the front pants slightly to fit the front band. Sew the front band to the top of the front pants with right sides together. Press open. Press the top edge of the band ¼" to the wrong side. Topstitch along the top and bottom edges a scant ⅛" from the edges.

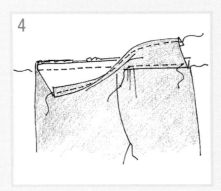

5 Serge or zigzag stitch the top of the back pants. Press ¾" to the wrong side and stitch ½" away from the pressed edge to create a casing. Thread elastic through this casing and secure the ends.

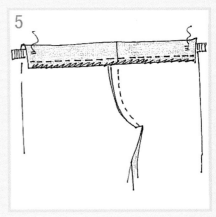

6 Sew the side seams with right sides together. Press.

7 Serge or zigzag stitch the lower edges of the pants. Press this edge ½" to the wrong side and stitch.

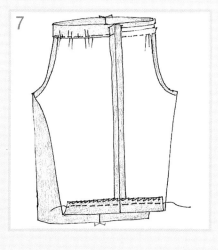

8 Sew the inner leg seam.

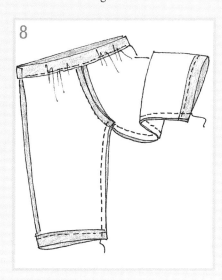

9 With right sides together, sew the bib to its lining along the top and both sides edges. Clip the corners; turn to the right side and press. Topstitch on these three edges a scant ⅛" from the edge.

10 Sew the pocket on the front of the bib as marked on the pattern piece. Pin the bib to the center of the front band with the lower edges of the bib extending ¼" below the top of the band. Stitch over the previous stitching to secure.

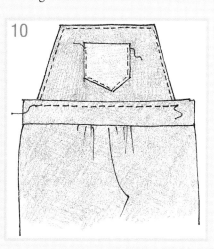

11 Press the long edges of each strap ¼" to the wrong side and stitch.

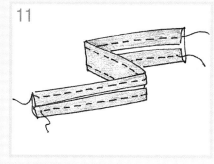

12 Stitch one of the raw ends of each strap to the back waistband approximately 1" (1", 1½", 1½") from the center back seam. The end should be tacked along the previous waistline stitching.

13 Place the buckle and slide on the other end following the instructions on the package. Attach the buttons to the bib as marked on the pattern piece. Cross the straps at the back and fasten on the front.

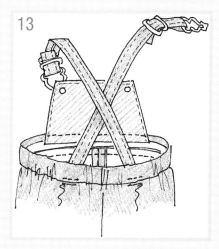

1 With right sides together, sew two fronts to one back at the shoulder seams. Repeat with the other fronts and back to make a lining. Press the seam allowances open.

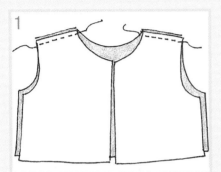

2 Fold the collar in half lengthwise with right sides together. Stitch across the short ends. Clip the corners; turn right side out and press.

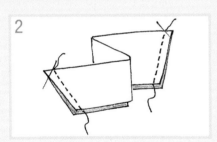

3 With right sides together, center the collar along the neckline of the shirt. Stitch. *Note:* The collar does not extend all the way to the center front edges.

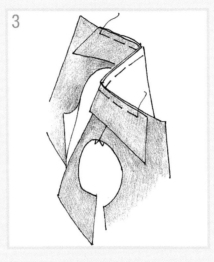

4 With right sides together, pin the shirt lining to the shirt, sandwiching the collar in between. Sew around the neckline, down the center fronts, and the bottom edges of both fronts and the back. Clip the curves; turn to the right side and press. Baste the lining to the shirt around the armholes.

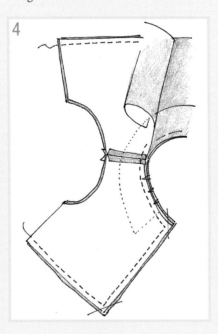

5 Serge or zigzag stitch the lower edge of the sleeves. Press the lower edge ¼" to the wrong side and stitch. Gather the sleeve caps between the dots. With right sides together, sew the sleeves to the armholes, easing in the sleeve.

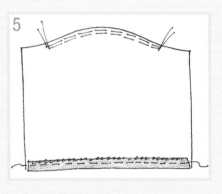

6 Sew the underarm seams from the cuff to the waist.

7 Lapping left over the right, sew the buttons to the left front as marked on the pattern piece. Sew the snaps underneath the buttons.

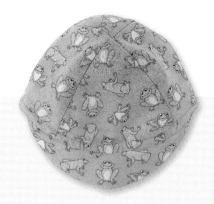

1 Sew the four cap sections together. Press the seam allowances to one side.

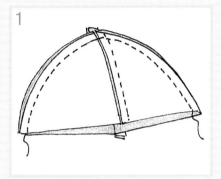

2 Place the brim interfacing on the wrong side of one of the brims and baste around the edges. Trim the interfacing along the outside of the stitching.

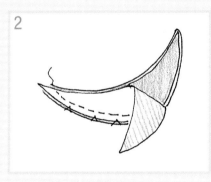

3 Sew the brims with right sides together along the outer curved edges. Clip the curves; trim the seam and turn to the right side. Press.

4 Center the brim along one of the cap sections and stitch with right sides together.

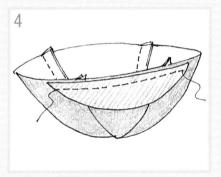

5 Beginning at the back of the cap, open out one side of the bias tape and stitch with right sides together along the lower edge of the cap, turning the beginning edge under ¼". When you have stitched all the way around, clip off the excess tape. Press the tape to the inside and stitch close to the other side of the bias tape.

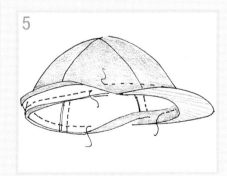

6 If cap does not fit snugly on the head, zigzag stitch a 1½"-2" piece of ⅛" elastic along the inside of the back of the hat.

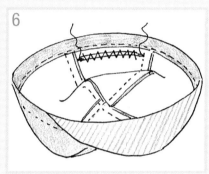

JUMPER, LONG-SLEEVED T-SHIRT AND WIDE-BRIMMED HAT

SUPPLIES

⅓ yd. (½ yd., ½ yd., ⅔ yd.) frog or other print fabric

¼ yd. (¼ yd., ⅓ yd., ⅓ yd) yellow knit fabric

Package of yellow baby rickrack

Set of overall buckles and slides*

Pair of overall buttons*

1½" x 6½" (7½", 9", 9½") yellow ribbing

4½" (5", 7½", 7½") elastic for the jumper, ⅜" wide

6" (7½", 8", 8") elastic for the sleeves, ⅛" wide

2" (3", 4", 4") Velcro strip

*Used in this project: Dritz for Dolls

CUTTING INSTRUCTIONS

From the print fabric, cut:
- Two jumper bibs (Pattern 48).
- Two jumper pockets (Pattern 49).
- Four hat sections (Pattern 14).
- Two hat brims (Pattern 50).
- One 1" x 5¾" (1¼" x 6½", 1¼" x 8½", 1¼" x 9") front band.
- Two 1" x 6¾" (8¾", 9½", 10¼") straps.
- One 4½" x 18" (5¾" x 20", 6½" x 20", 8" x 22½") front skirt.
- One 5¼" x 18" (6½" x 20", 7¼" x 20", 8¾" x 22½") back skirt.

From the yellow knit fabric, cut:
- One shirt front (Pattern 9).
- Two shirt backs (Pattern 10).
- Two shirt sleeves (Pattern 8).

1 Gather one long edge of the front skirt to fit the front band. With right sides together, sew the front band to the skirt front. Press open. Press the top edge of the band ¼" to the wrong side. Topstitch along the top and bottom edges a scant ⅛" from the edges.

2 Serge or zigzag stitch the top of the back skirt. Press ¾" to the wrong side and stitch ½" away from the pressed edge to create a casing. Thread elastic through this casing and secure the ends.

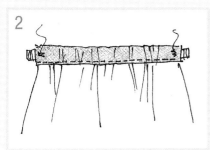

3 With right sides together, sew the side seams. Serge or zigzag stitch the lower edge of the skirt. Press this edge ¾" to the wrong side.

4 Sew the rickrack to the skirt ½" from the pressed edge, catching the hem in the stitching.

5 With right sides together, sew the bib and its lining along the side and top edges. Clip the curves; turn to the right side and press. Topstitch on these three edges a scant ⅛" from the edge.

6 Cut a piece of rickrack to fit across the pocket. Sew the rickrack ¾" from the top of the pocket. With right sides together, sew the pockets together, leaving a small opening. Clip the corners; turn to the right side and press.

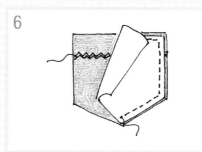

7 Sew the pocket to the bib as marked on the pattern piece.

8 Pin the bib to the center of the front band with the lower edges of the bib extending ¼" below the top of the band. Stitch over the previous stitching to secure.

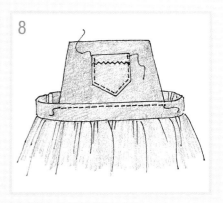

9 Press the long edges of each strap ¼" to the wrong side and stitch.

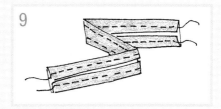

10 Stitch one of the raw ends of each strap to the back waistband approximately 1" (1", 1½", 1½") from the center back seam. The end should be tacked along the previous waistline stitching. Attach the buckle and slide on the other end following the instructions on the package. Attach the buttons on the bib as marked on the pattern piece. Cross the straps at the back and fasten on the front.

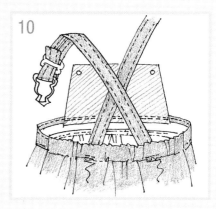

LONG-SLEEVED T-SHIRT

LONG-SLEEVED T-SHIRT

1 Press the center back edges ¼" to the wrong side and stitch.

2 With right sides together, sew the shoulder seams with serger or zigzag stitch.

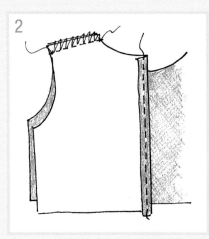

3 Fold the neckline ribbing in half lengthwise with right sides together. Stitch the short ends and turn to the right side. Stretching the ribbing to fit the neckline, serge or zigzag stitch the ribbing to the neckline.

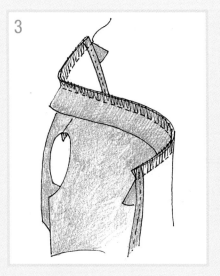

4 Narrow-hem the bottom of each sleeve edge. Cut the sleeve elastic in half. Starting at one side of the sleeve and ½" from the hemmed edge, sew the sleeve elastic by zigzag stitching over the top, stretching the elastic to the other side of the sleeve. Do not catch the elastic in your stitching except to secure the ends at each side.

5 Gather the sleeve caps between the dots marked on the pattern piece. With right sides together, sew the sleeve caps to the armholes.

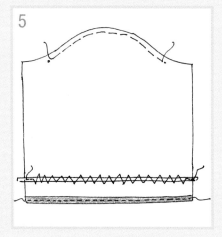

6 Sew the underarm seam.

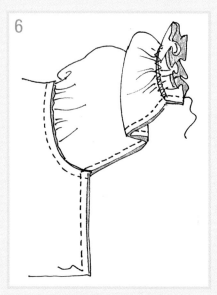

7 Serge or zigzag stitch the lower edge of the shirt. Press the edge ⅜" to the wrong side and topstitch.

8 Lapping right over left, sew the Velcro to the back opening.

1 Sew the hat sections together.

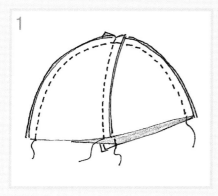

2 Sew the ends of each brim with right sides together. Stitch the brims with right sides together along the outside edges. Clip the curves; turn to the right side and press.

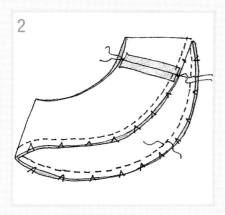

3 Sew the raw edges of the brim to the right side of the lower hat edge.

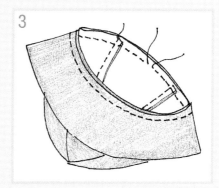

4 Topstitch along the hat a scant ⅛" from the hat/brim seam, catching the seam allowance in the stitching. Sew the rickrack to the underside of the brim ½" from the outside edge, overlapping the ends. Fold the brim up in the front.

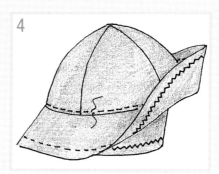

Tees for Two

MAXI-MUFFIN BY GÖTZ

These twin cuties sport matching T-shirt knit dresses with knit jackets. The quick and easy dresses are sewn from stretchy T-shirt knit prints with tailored sleeves and Peter Pan collars. Choose prints or stripes that are scaled small enough for doll clothing. The jackets can be made from stretch terry fabric or other knits to insure a good fit. Decorate the front opening with any of your decorative machine stitches, rickrack or other fun trims available today.

T-SHIRT DRESS
AND JACKET

SUPPLIES

⅓ yd. (½ yd., ½ yd., ⅔ yd.) print knit fabric for the dress

¼ yd. (¼ yd., ⅓ yd., ⅓ yd.) stretch terry fabric for the jacket

Package of matching color single fold bias tape

3" (4", 4", 5") Velcro strip

Package baby rickrack (optional)

Decorative machine embroidery thread (optional)

CUTTING INSTRUCTIONS

From the print knit fabric, cut:
• One bodice front (Pattern 9).
• Two bodice backs (Pattern 10).
• Two dress sleeves (Pattern 25).
• Four dress collars (Pattern 18).
• One 4" x 30" (5" x 30", 6¼" x 45", 7¾" x 45") skirt.

From the stretch terry fabric, cut:
• Two jacket fronts (Pattern 37).
• One jacket back (Pattern 38).
• Two jacket sleeves (Pattern 25).

T-SHIRTDRESS

MAXI-MUFFIN BY GÖTZ

1 With right sides together, sew the backs to the front at the shoulders.

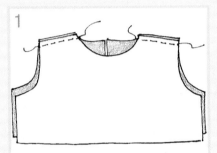

2 Sew two collar pieces with right sides together around the outside curved edge. Clip the curves; turn to the right side and press. Repeat with the remaining collar pieces.

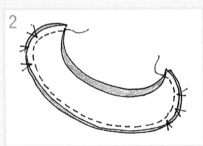

3 Pin the collars along the outside edge of the neckline so they meet at the center front. Baste in place. *Note:* They do not extend all the way to the back edges.

4 Open out one side of the bias tape and pin it to the neckline with right sides together, extending the short ends by ¼", and cutting off the excess. Stitch. Fold the bias tape to the inside and stitch, tucking in the short ends. Be sure to keep the collars away from the stitching.

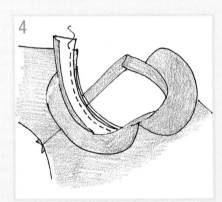

5 Serge or zigzag stitch the lower sleeve edges. Press this edge ¼" to the wrong side and stitch.

6 Sew the sleeve caps to the armholes, easing as necessary.

7 Sew the underarm seam from the sleeve edge to the bottom of the bodice.

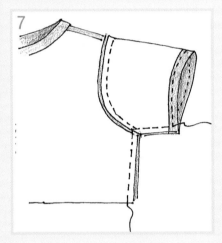

8 Serge or zigzag stitch the two short ends and one long edge of the skirt. Press each of the ends and the long edge ½" to the wrong side and stitch. Gather the remaining long edge of the skirt to fit the bodice and stitch with right sides together.

9 Lapping right over left, sew the Velcro to the back opening.

1 With right sides together, sew the fronts to the back at the shoulders. Press the seam allowances open.

2 Serge or zigzag stitch the neckline. Press it ⅜" to the wrong side and stitch.

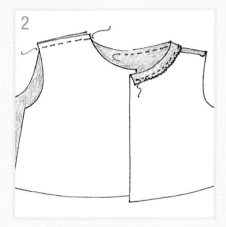

3 Serge or zigzag stitch the lower edges of the sleeves. Press them ¼" to the wrong side and stitch.

4 Sew the sleeve caps to the armholes, easing as necessary.

5 Sew the underarm seam from the sleeve edge to the bottom of the jacket.

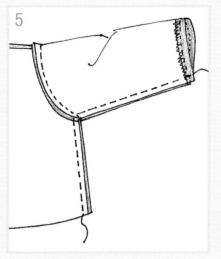

6 Serge or zigzag stitch the lower edge of the jacket. Press it ⅜" to the wrong side and stitch.

7 Press the front edges of the jacket ½" to the wrong side. Stitch along the front edges by sewing two rows of decorative machine stitches or two rows of baby rickrack along the front edges.

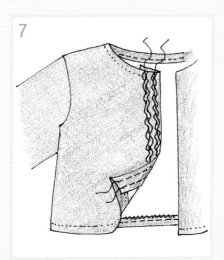

MAXI-MUFFIN BY GÖTZ

MAXI-MUFFIN BY GÖTZ

Summer Fruit

ZAPF CREATION AND GÖTZ

Summer fruits can be fashioned into charming dresses and caps for baby dolls. Pink and green print fabrics work well for strawberry and watermelon outfits. The dresses are both the same with puffed sleeves and gathered skirts, and the panties have elastic at the waist and leg openings. The collars differ to signify the different fruits. The strawberry dress has many separate green petals, while the watermelon has a round pink, green and white collar with black "seeds."

STRAWBERRY DRESS, PANTIES AND CAP

SUPPLIES

⅓ yd. (½ yd., ⅔ yd., ⅔ yd.) pink solid or print cotton fabric

¼ yd. (⅓ yd., ½ yd., ½ yd.) green solid or print cotton fabric

8" (8", 11", 11") elastic for the sleeves, ⅛" wide

10½" (12", 14", 16") elastic for the leg openings, ⅛" wide

8" (11", 14", 17") elastic for the waist, ⅜" wide

Scrap of darker green cotton fabric for the "stem" on the cap

2" (3", 4", 4") Velcro strip

1½"-2" elastic, ⅛" wide (optional)

CUTTING INSTRUCTIONS

From the pink cotton fabric, cut:
- Two bodice fronts (Pattern 16).
- Four bodice backs (Pattern 17).
- Two dress sleeves (Pattern 8).
- Four cap sections (Pattern 14).
- One 5½" x 36" (6¼" x 40", 6¾" x 45", 7¾" x 45") skirt.

From the green cotton fabric, cut:
- 12 petals (Pattern 51).
- Four panties (Pattern 7).
- One 2½" x 12" (3" x 14", 3½" x 15", 3½" x 18") band.

From the scrap of darker green cotton fabric, cut:
- One ¾" x 2" stem.

STRAWBERRY DRESS

STRAWBERRY DRESS

1 With the right sides together, sew a front to two backs at the shoulders. Press the seam allowances open. Repeat with the remaining pieces for the lining and set aside.

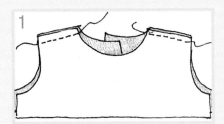

2 Sew two of the petals right sides together around the outside curved edge. Clip the curves; turn to the right side and press. Repeat with the remaining petals.

3 Place the petals along the neckline edge so they slightly overlap. They should stop approximately ¾" from the center back edges. Baste in place.

4 With right sides together, sew the lining to the dress bodice along one center back, around the neckline, and down the other center back, sandwiching the petals in between. Clip the curves and turn to the right side. Press.

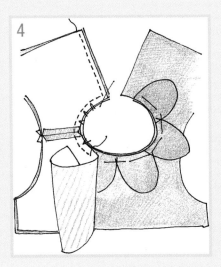

5 Baste the armholes of the lining and the dress bodice together.

6 Narrow-hem the bottom of each sleeve edge. Cut the sleeve elastic in half. Starting at one side of the sleeve and ½" from the hemmed edge, sew the sleeve elastic by zigzag stitching over the top, stretching the elastic to the other side of the sleeve. Do not catch the elastic in your stitching except to secure the ends at each side. Gather the sleeve caps between the dots marked on the pattern piece.

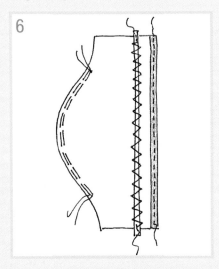

7 With right sides together, sew the sleeve caps to the armholes. Sew the underarm seam.

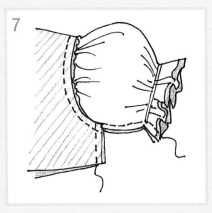

8 Press the two short ends of the skirt ¼" to the wrong side and stitch. Press one long edge ¼" to the wrong side. Press another ½" and stitch.

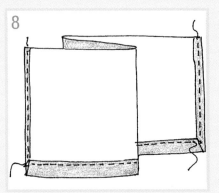

9 Gather the top edge of the skirt and stitch to the bodice with right sides together.

10 Lapping right over left, sew the Velcro to the back opening.

1 With right sides together, sew the center front and center back seams of the panties. Sew the side seams with right sides together.

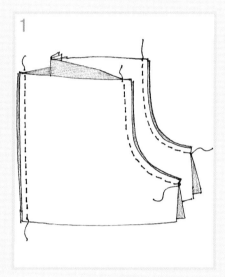

2 Narrow-hem the lower edges of the legs. Cut the leg opening elastic in half. Starting at one side of the leg opening and ½" from the hemmed edge, sew the leg elastic by zigzag stitching over the top, stretching the elastic to the other side of the leg opening. Do not catch the elastic in your stitching except to secure the ends at each side.

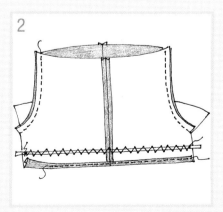

3 Sew the inner leg seam.

4 Serge or zigzag stitch the top edge of the panties. Press this edge ¾" to the wrong side and stitch ½" from the folded edge to form a casing, leaving a small opening in the back. Thread the waistband elastic through this casing and secure the ends. Stitch the opening closed.

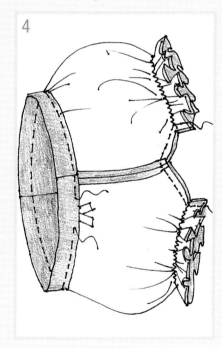

1 Sew the cap sections together, leaving a small opening at the top to insert the stem. Press the seams to one side.

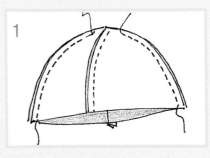

2 With right sides together, sew the short ends of the band and turn to the right side. Fold the band in half lengthwise with wrong sides together and press.

3 Stitch the band to the wrong side of the lower edge of the cap. Fold the band to the outside of the cap and press.

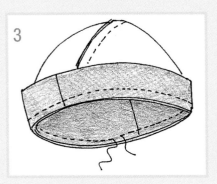

4 Press the long sides of the stem ¼" to the wrong side. Fold it in half again to make a narrow tube and hand stitch together.

5 Fold the stem in half widthwise and insert it into the opening in the top of the cap. Hand tack it in place, making sure to stitch the seams in the cap closed.

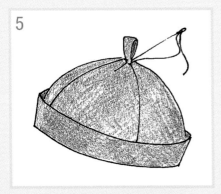

6 If the cap doesn't fit snugly on the head, zigzag stitch a 1½"-2" piece of ⅛" wide elastic along the inside of the back of the cap.

WATERMELON DRESS, CAP AND PANTIES

SUPPLIES

⅓ yd. (½ yd., ⅔ yd., ⅔ yd.) green solid or print cotton fabric

¼ yd. (⅓ yd., ½ yd., ½ yd.) pink solid or print cotton fabric

Package of single fold white bias tape

Package of extra wide, double fold, green bias tape

10-25 black beads, size 3mm

8" (8", 11", 11") elastic for the sleeves, ⅛" wide

10½", (12", 14", 16") elastic for the leg openings, ⅛" wide

8", (11", 14", 17") elastic for the waist, ⅜" wide

Scrap of darker green cotton fabric for the "stem" on the cap

White thread

CUTTING INSTRUCTIONS

From the green cotton fabric, cut:
- •Four cap sections (Pattern 14).
- •Two bodice fronts (Pattern 16).
- •Four bodice backs (Pattern 17).
- •Two dress sleeves (Pattern 8).
- •One 5½" x 36" (6¼" x 40", 6¾" x 45", 7¾" x 45") skirt.

From the pink cotton fabric, cut:
- •Four panties (Pattern 7).
- •One collar (Pattern 52).
- •One 2½" x 12" (3" x 14", 3½" x 15", 3½" x 18") band.

WATERMELON DRESS

WATERMELON DRESS

1 With the right sides together, sew a front to two backs at the shoulders. Press the seam allowances open. Repeat with the remaining pieces for the lining and set aside.

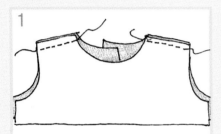

2 Pin one side of the white bias tape just above the lower edge of the collar. Stitch with white thread and cut off the excess.

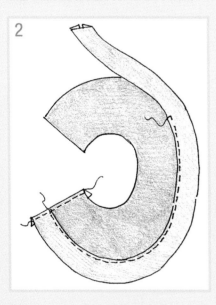

3 Press the back straight edges of the collar ¼" to the wrong side and stitch.

4 Cut a piece of green bias tape to fit the bottom of the collar, extending each end by ¼". Pin the tape to the collar, enclosing the lower edge of the white bias tape inside the folds. Stitch the tape to the collar, tucking in the short ends at each side of the collar.

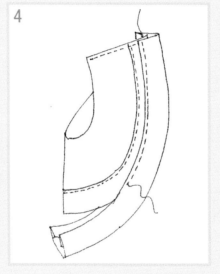

5 Baste the collar to the neckline. *Note:* The collar does not extend all the way to the center back edges.

6 With right sides together, sew the lining to the dress bodice along one center back, around the neckline, and down the other center back, sandwiching the collar in between. Clip the curves and turn to the right side. Press.

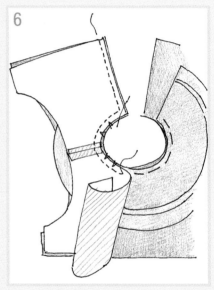

7 Baste the armholes of the lining and dress bodice together.

8 Follow Steps 6-10 from the Strawberry Dress on page 66.

9 Randomly sew the beads to the collar, using as many as necessary to fill the collar with "seeds," as shown in the photo.

CAP

Make the cap following the instructions for the Strawberry Cap on page 68.

PANTIES

Make the panties following the instructions for the Strawberry Panties on page 67.

 Use bright yellow and orange fabrics to adapt this outfit for citrus fruits. Use the same round collar, but with white stitching to resemble citrus segments.

COROLLE AND FISHER-PRICE

Fresh as a Daisy

LEE MIDDLETON

Bright and sunny daisy prints are just the right scale for doll clothing. This yellow and orange daisy print dress has a contrasting collar with orange piping and short puffed sleeves. The sash has daisy lace trim applied to the front and ties in the back. The centers of the daisy trim can be colored to match any dress fabric with a fabric marker (if the trim will not be washed). The panties are from the same fabric with elastic at the waist and leg openings. The headband with an orange bow is made from a long fabric tube with elastic in the center.

DAISY DRESS, PANTIES AND HEADBAND

SUPPLIES

½ yd. (½ yd., ⅔ yd., ⅔ yd.) daisy or other print cotton fabric

Scrap of white fabric for the collar

Package of purchased piping

8" (8", 11", 11") elastic for the sleeves, ⅛" wide

10½" (12", 14", 16") elastic for the leg openings, ⅛" wide

8" (11", 14", 17") elastic for the waist, ⅜" wide

10½" (12½", 13½", 14") elastic for the headband, ½" wide

⅔ yd. (1 yd., 1 yd., 1 yd.) satin ribbon for the sash, ⅝" (1", 1", 1") wide

⅓ yd. satin ribbon for the bow on the headband, ⅝" (1", 1", 1") wide

¼ yd. daisy trim, ⅝" (⅞", ⅞", ⅞") wide

3" (3", 4", 4") Velcro strip

CUTTING INSTRUCTIONS

From the print cotton fabric, cut:
- Two dress fronts (Pattern 16).
- Four dress backs (Pattern 17).
- Two dress sleeves (Pattern 8).
- Four panties (Pattern 7).
- One 5½" x 36" (6¼" x 40", 6¾" x 45", 7¾" x 45") skirt.
- One 1½" x 17" (2" x 20", 2" x 25", 2" x 28") headband strip.

From the white fabric, cut:
- Four collars (Pattern 18).

DAISY DRESS

DAISY DRESS

1 With the right sides together, sew a front to two backs at the shoulders. Press the seam allowances open. Repeat with the remaining pieces for the lining.

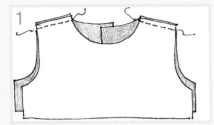

2 Baste the piping to the outside edge of one of the collar pieces. Place another collar piece on top and stitch with right sides together. Trim the seam allowance; clip the curves and turn to the right side. Press. Repeat with the remaining collar pieces.

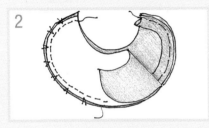

3 Pin the collars to the neckline of the dress so they meet at the center front. Baste. *Note:* They do not extend to the back opening.

4 With right sides together, sew the lining to the dress bodice along one center back, around the neckline, and down the other center back, sandwiching the collar in between. Clip the curves and turn to the right side. Press.

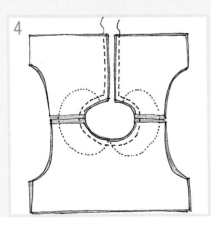

5 Baste the armholes together.

6 Narrow-hem the bottom of each sleeve edge. Cut the sleeve elastic in half. Starting at one side of the sleeve and ½" from the hemmed edge, sew the sleeve elastic by zigzag stitching over the top, stretching the elastic to the other side of the sleeve. Do not catch the elastic in your stitching except to secure the ends at each side. Gather the sleeve caps between the dots marked on the pattern piece.

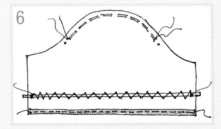

7 With right sides together, sew the sleeve caps to the armholes. Sew the underarm seam.

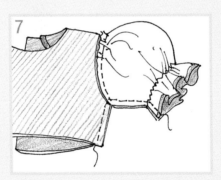

8 Press the two short ends of the skirt ¼" to the wrong side and stitch. Press one long edge ¼" to the wrong side, press another ½" and stitch.

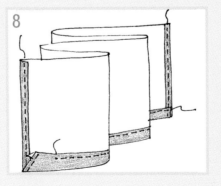

9 Gather the top edge of the skirt and stitch to the bodice with right sides together.

10 Lapping right over left, sew the Velcro to the back opening.

11 For the sash, place the daisy trim in the center of the sash ribbon and hand stitch it in place, trimming any excess lace that extends beyond the side seams of the dress. Tie the sash around the waist with a bow at the back.

1 With right sides together, sew the center front and center back seams of the panties. Sew the side seams with right sides together.

3 Sew the inner leg seam.

4 Serge or zigzag stitch the top edge of the panties. Press this edge ¾" to the wrong side and stitch ½" from the folded edge to form a casing, leaving a small opening in the back. Thread the waistband elastic through this casing and secure the ends. Stitch the opening closed.

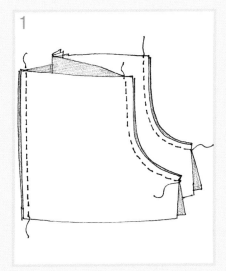

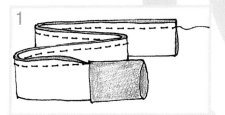

2 Narrow-hem the lower edges of the panty legs. Cut the leg opening elastic in half. Sew the elastic ½" above the hemmed edge, zigzag stitching over the top, stretching the elastic to the other side of the sleeve. Do not catch the elastic in your stitching except to secure the ends at each side.

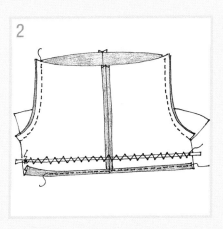

1 Fold the headband strip in half lengthwise with right sides together and stitch. Turn to the right side.

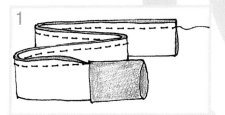

2 Thread the headband elastic through the tube and stitch at each end to secure. Sew the fabric ends together.

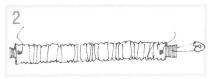

3 Tie the ribbon for the headband into a bow and tack it to the front of the center of the headband.

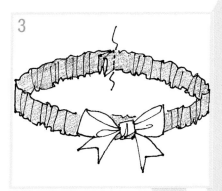

Sleepytime

BITTY BABY TWINS BY PLEASANT COMPANY

Bedtime for your dolls can be fun in these beary cute knit pajamas! The girl's nightshirt has a fast and easy bear appliqué from the knit print fabric, while the boy's pajamas have a bear appliqué made from felt. Their caps have a rolled brim with "ears" sewn in the seams. The slippers worn by the girl doll have knit ribbing cut to fit the ankles and a ribbon bow on the top. Make a pair for boys by eliminating the bow.

NIGHTSHIRT, CAP AND SLIPPERS

SUPPLIES

⅓ yd. (½ yd., ½ yd., ⅔ yd.) pink knit fabric

¼ yd. print knit fabric

1½" x 6½" (7½", 9", 9½") strip of blue ribbing for the neckline

2 strips of blue ribbing 1¾" x 3" (3½", 4½", 4½") for the cuffs

4" (5", 5", 6") Velcro strip

Scrap of tan felt for the bear's jowls

Fusible web

Pink embroidery floss

2 black beads, size 4mm

Temporary spray adhesive

Fabric glue

½ yd. pink ribbon, ⅛" wide

CUTTING INSTRUCTIONS

From the pink knit fabric, cut:
- One nightshirt front (Pattern 53).
- Two nightshirt backs (Pattern 54).
- Two nightshirt sleeves (Pattern 25).
- One 2½" x 12" (3" x 14", 3½" x 15", 3½" x 18") strip for the cap band.
- Two 1¾" x 4" (2" x 5", 2" x 5½", 2" x 5½") slipper cuffs.

From the print knit fabric, cut:
- One bear head (Pattern 55).
- Four cap sections (Pattern 14).
- Four ears (Pattern 56).
- Two slipper uppers (Pattern 21).
- Two slipper soles (Pattern 23).

From the tan felt:
- *Note:* Leave room for one jowls (Pattern 57). See Step 10.

NIGHTSHIRT

NIGHTSHIRT

1 Serge or zigzag stitch the raw edge of the front from the armhole, around the curved hem, and stopping at the other armhole. Do not cut any fabric from the seam allowance as you stitch. Repeat with the backs.

2 With right sides together, sew the backs to the front at the shoulder seams.

3 Zigzag stitch or serge the center back seams. Press ¼" to the wrong side and stitch.

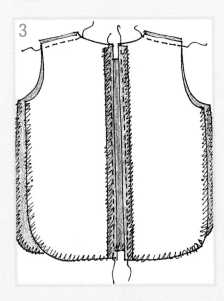

4 Fold the neckline ribbing in half lengthwise with right sides together. Stitch the short ends and turn to the right side.

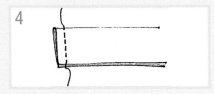

5 Stretching the ribbing to fit the neckline, serge or zigzag stitch the ribbing to the neckline.

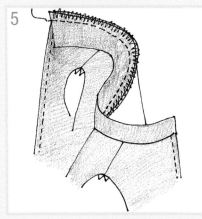

6 Fold each piece of the cuff ribbing in half lengthwise with wrong sides together. Stretch the cuffs to fit the lower edge of each sleeve and zigzag stitch or serge.

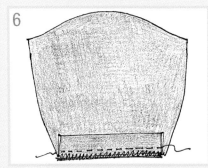

7 With right sides together, sew the sleeve caps to the armholes, easing to fit.

8 Stitch the underarm seam, beginning at the sleeve edge and stopping at the dot marked on the front and back pattern pieces. Press the seam allowances open.

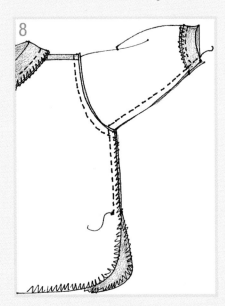

9 Press the curved hem edge ⅜" to the wrong side and topstitch around the hem.

10 For the bear appliqué, trace the jowls onto the tan felt, but do not cut out. Embroider the nose with a satin stitch and mouth lines with a back stitch by hand on the pink felt jowls.

11 Cut out the jowls and glue to the bear head.

12 Spray the back of the head with temporary adhesive spray and place on the front of the nightshirt as marked on the pattern piece. Stitch very close to the outer edge of the appliqué with a straight stitch.

CAP

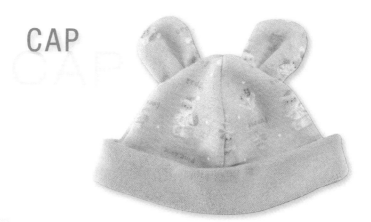

13 Sew the two beads above the jowls with black thread for the eyes.

14 Lapping right over left, sew the Velcro to the back opening.

1 With right sides together, sew two of the ears together along the curved outside edge. Clip the curves; turn to the right side and press. Repeat with the remaining ears.

2 Make a small pleat along the raw bottom edges of one ear so the bottom edge measures ¾" (1", 1", 1"). Repeat with the remaining ear.

3 With right sides together, sew two cap sections together along the sides. Repeat with the remaining two sections.

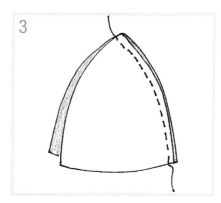

4 Pin the ears along the right side of one of the stitched cap halves as marked on the pattern piece. With right sides together, sew the cap halves together.

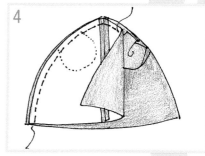

5 Sew the short ends of the pink band with right sides together.

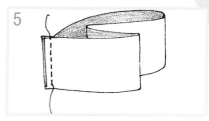

6 Fold the band in half lengthwise with wrong sides together. Stitch the raw edges of band to the wrong side of the bottom of the cap. Fold over to the right side.

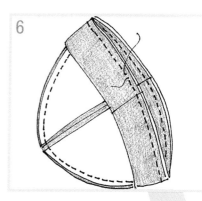

SLIPPERS

SLIPPERS

1 Fold the cuff lengthwise with wrong sides together. Stitch the raw edges to the curved inside edge of the slipper upper. Repeat with the remaining cuff and slipper upper.

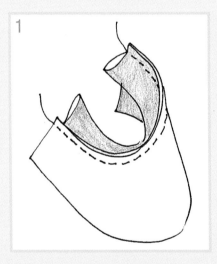

2 With right sides together, sew the heel seam of each upper.

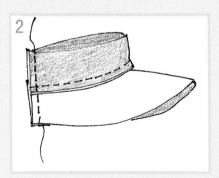

3 Stitch the upper to the sole. Clip the curves and turn to the right side. Repeat with the other upper.

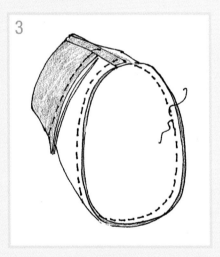

4 Make two bows with the ribbon and tack one to the front of each slipper on the cuff/upper seam.

PAJAMA TOP, CAP AND PAJAMA PANTS

SUPPLIES

⅓ yd. (½ yd., ½ yd., ⅔ yd.) print knit fabric

8" (11", 14", 17") elastic, ⅜" wide

⅛ yd. tan ribbing for the pajama top

2" (4", 4", 5") Velcro strip

Scrap of tan felt for the bear head

Scrap of pink felt for the bear's jowls

Pink embroidery floss

2 black beads, 4mm

Fabric glue

⅛ yd. blue ribbing for the cap banding

CUTTING INSTRUCTIONS

From the print knit fabric, cut:
• One top front (Pattern 9).
• Two top backs (Pattern 10).
• Two sleeves (Pattern 25).
• Four pants (Pattern 26).
• Four cap sections (Pattern 14).
• Four ears (Pattern 56).

From the tan ribbing, cut:
• One 1½" x 6½" (7½", 9", 9½") strip for the neckline.
• Two 1½" x 3" (3½", 4½", 4½") strips for the sleeve cuffs.
• Two 1½" x 4" (1½" x 4", 2" x 5½", 2" x 5½") strips for the pant cuffs.

From the blue ribbing, cut:
• 2½" x 12" (3" x 14", 3½" x 15", 3½" x 18") for the cap banding.

From the tan felt, cut:
• One bear head (Pattern 55).

From the pink felt:
• *Note:* Leave room for one jowls (Pattern 57). See Step 7.

1 Sew the front to the backs with right sides together. Zigzag stitch or serge the center back seams. Press ¼" to the wrong side and stitch.

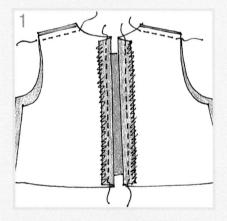

2 Fold the tan ribbing strip for the neckline in half lengthwise with right sides together. Stitch the short ends and turn to the right side.

3 Stretching the ribbing to fit the neckline, serge or zigzag stitch the ribbing to the neckline.

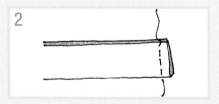

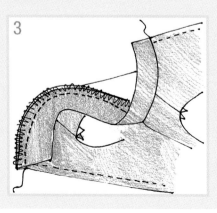

4 Fold each piece of the cuff ribbing in half lengthwise with wrong sides together. Stretch the cuffs to fit the lower edge of each sleeve and zigzag stitch or serge. With right sides together, sew the sleeve caps to the armholes, easing to fit.

5 Stitch the underarm seam, beginning at the sleeve edge and ending at the bottom of the pajama top.

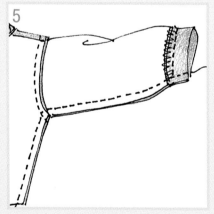

6 Serge or zigzag stitch the bottom of the pajama top and press ⅜" to the wrong side. Stitch ¼" from the folded edge.

7 Trace the jowls onto the pink felt, but do not cut them out. Embroider the nose with a satin stitch and mouth lines with a back stitch by hand on the pink felt jowls.

8 Cut out the jowls and glue to the bear head.

9 Sew the beads above the jowls for the eyes.

10 Glue the bear head on the front of the pajama top with fabric glue, as marked on the pattern piece.

11 Lapping right over left, sew the Velcro to the back opening.

CAP

Make the cap following the instructions for the cap with the Nightshirt on page 79.

PAJAMA PANTS

1 With right sides together, sew the center front and center back seams of the pants. Sew the side seams with right sides together.

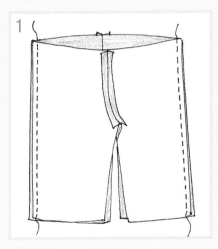

2 Fold each piece of tan ribbing for the pant cuffs in half lengthwise with wrong sides together and stitch to the bottom of each pant leg, stretching to fit.

3 Sew the inner leg seam.

4 Serge or zigzag stitch the top of the pants and press ¾" to the wrong side. Stitch ½" from the pressed edge to form a casing, leaving a 1" opening at the back. Thread the elastic through the casing and secure the ends. Stitch the opening closed.

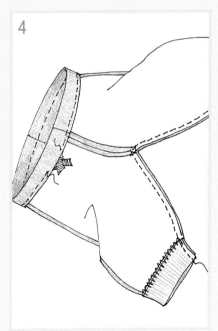

Butterfly Kisses

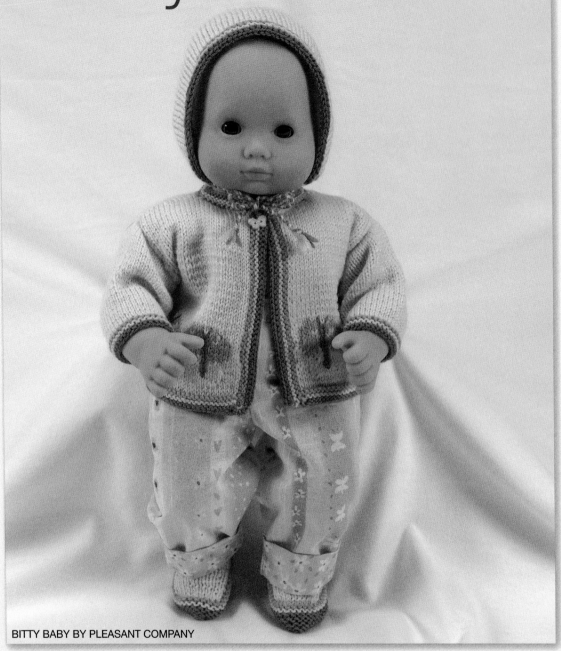

BITTY BABY BY PLEASANT COMPANY

A knitted sweater with matching cap and booties is a baby doll wardrobe staple. This set has charming little butterflies knit along the lower edge of the sweater. The bodies of the butterflies are done with duplicate stitch since they are so small. The sweater closes at the neck with a snap and a decorative butterfly button on top. You can decide to knit in buttonholes if you prefer (as usual with knitted items, if you have difficulty in getting a proper fit, try a different needle size or adjust the gauge). The pants have cuffs at the ankles made from a contrasting print fabric.

CAP, BOOTIES, SWEATER AND CUFFED PANTS

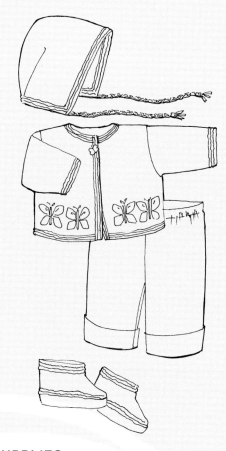

CAP

In main body color, cast on 18 (18, 30, 30) sts. Work in stockinette st for 3" (3", 3¾", 3¾"). Bind off. Pick up 18 (18, 20, 20) sts on side, 18 (18, 20, 20) across the top and 18 (18, 20, 20) along the other side. Knit in stockinette st until piece measures 2½" (2½", 3", 3").

With color #3, knit across all sts. Pick up 44 (44, 46, 46) sts across the bottom edge, pick up every other st, then do the other side piece the same as the first. Knit one more row with color #3, two rows with color #2, and one row with color #1. Bind off in color #1.

TIES

Measure 12" of yarn in each of the contrasting colors. With crochet hook, thread all three colors through the corners of the cap. Pull through so the hat corner marks the halfway mark of the ties. Braid ties and tie a knot at the end of the braid.

BOOTIES

Beginning a top of bootie with color #1, cast on 30 sts for all sizes. Knit one more round. With color #2, knit two rows. With color #3, knit two rows.

With main body color, work 6 rows in stockinette st. Work center 10 st for 4 (4, 10, 10) rows. Break yarn.

Join yarn at heel, knit 10 sts, pick up 2 (2, 6, 6) sts on side of center 10 sts, knit center 10 sts, pick up 2 (2, 10, 10) sts on the other side of the toe piece, knit remaining 10 sts to end of row.

Break yarn. With right side facing, start again at beginning of row with color #3. Knit two rows 34 (34, 40, 40) sts. Knit two rows in color #2. Knit 5 (5, 14, 14) rows with color #3. Bind off. Sew the bottom of the bootie and heel together.

SUPPLIES:

2 balls (50 gm) of fingering weight yarn in the main body color (for large and x-large sizes, you may want to try a slightly heavier yarn, such as sport weight)

50 gm ball of fingering weight yarn in three contrasting colors

Knitting needles, size 2

Butterfly button, size ½"

Small snap

Stitch holder

Crochet hook, size C or D

Gauge for small: 7 sts per inch in stockinette stitch

Gauge for medium: 6½ sts per inch in stockinette stitch

Gauge for large and x-large: 6½ sts per inch in stockinette stitch

BUTTERFLY SWEATER

BUTTERFLY SWEATER

(DESIGNED BY LAURI CUSHING)

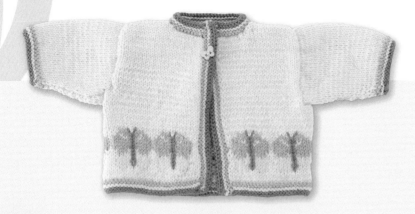

BODY

Cast on 90 (90, 112, 112) stitches with color #1, knit one row. With color #2 knit two rows. With color #3 knit two rows. Using main color, work in stockinette st (knit one row, purl one row) for 4 (4, 6, 6) rows, then work pattern chart according to size. Work in stockinette st until piece measures 3 (3, 3¾, 3¾) inches ending with a wrong side row.

DIVIDE FOR SLEEVES
LEFT UPPER FRONT

Knit 23 (23, 28, 28), turn work, bind off 2 (2, 3, 3) sts and work on remaining 21 (21, 25, 25) sts until entire measurement is 4" (4", 5¼", 5¼").

Next row (right side) bind off 8 (8, 9, 9) sts for the neck. Decrease 1 st at neck edge every other row x3 (x3, x2, x2), ending with wrong side row. For small size only, knit 7 more rows. (This is due to a deeper curve of the neck. Check the front to your doll and see if you need to add extra rows.) For all sizes, break yarn and put remaining 10 (10, 14, 14) stitches on a holder.

UPPER BACK

Working on next 44 (44, 56, 56) sts, bind off 2 (2, 3, 3) sts at the beginning of next two rows. Work until back measures the same as the front. Put 10 (10, 14, 14) sts at each sleeve side on holder for shoulder and the remaining 20 (20, 22, 22) sts on a holder for the neck.

RIGHT UPPER FRONT

Work as for left upper front, but reverse the bind offs and dec.

SHOULDERS

Take the 10 (10, 14, 14) sts from the back and the 10 (10, 14, 14) sts from the front and put them on two needles. Hold right sides together and do double bind off. (Take one st from the front needle and one from the back and knit them together. Do the next two sts the same way and then pull first st over second st which is just binding off. Continue until you run out of sts.

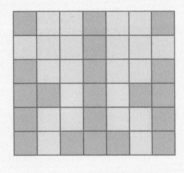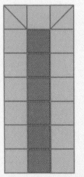

Graph for duplicate stitch.

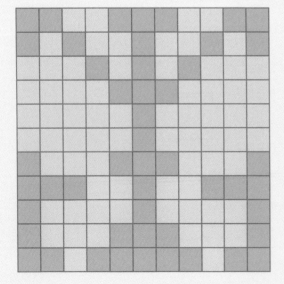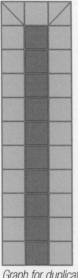

Graph for duplicate stitch.

NECK BANDS

With color #3, pick up and knit 16 (11, 11, 11) sts from side neck, 20 (20, 22, 22) from back neck, and 16 (11, 11, 11) from the other side neck. (The small size has more sts on the side necks due to extra rows knitted on the fronts.) Knit one more row in color #3, then two rows in color #2, and one row in color #1. Bind off in color #1.

BANDS

Starting at lower right front, pick up 34 (34, 44, 44) sts including neck rib. Starting with color #3, work the same as neck band. Repeat for band on left front.

SLEEVES

(make two sleeves)
Using color #1, cast on 34 sts for all sizes. Work the same as sweater body. For small and medium sizes, knit straight up for 4" in body color and bind off. For large and x-large sizes, on right side row increase 4 sts evenly (38 sts). Purl next row. Increase one st at each end of next row and then again for every 4th row until sleeve measures 3" (4", 6¼", 6¼") and there are 48 sts on the needle. Purl one more row. Bind off 3 sts at the beginning of next 6 rows, then bind off entire row. For all sizes, sew the sleeve seam and then sew the sleeve into the armhole.

Work duplicate sts in the bodies of the butterflies. Block and sew a butterfly button at neck with a snap underneath.

SUPPLIES

⅓ yd. (⅓ yd., ½ yd., ½ yd.) cotton print fabric to match sweater

8" (11", 14", 17") elastic, ⅜" wide

1¾" x 14" (2" x 17", 2" x 19", 2½" x 20") piece of contrasting print fabric for cuffs

CUTTING INSTRUCTIONS

From the cotton print fabric, cut:
• Four pants (Pattern 26).

1 With right sides together, sew the side seams and the center front and back seams.

2 Cut the contrasting fabric strip in half widthwise. Fold each strip in half lengthwise with wrong sides together and press. Stitch the right side of the cuff to the wrong side of each pant leg. Fold the cuff over to the right side and press.

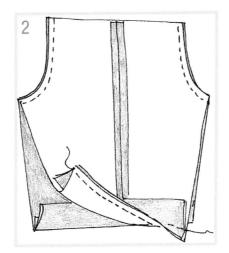

3 Serge or zigzag stitch the top edge of the pants. Press the top edge of the pants ¾" to the wrong side. Stitch ½" from the folded edge to form a casing, leaving a 1" opening in the back. Thread the elastic through the casing and secure the ends. Stitch the opening closed.

4 Sew the inner leg seam.

Warm and Cozy

ZAPF CREATION

This cardigan is knit with three colors of yarn in a checkerboard pattern along the lower edge. It has heart buttons in the front. The stripes in the stocking cap mimic the stripes in the sleeves. The elastic-waist pants in matching cobalt blue twill fabric are quick and easy to sew.

CARDIGAN, PANTS AND STOCKING CAP

If the color changes in the instructions for this sweater seem difficult to understand, look closely at the photograph to see what the final result should be. This should help you visualize what you are knitting. The center front bands are worked along with the sweater in seed stitch* with yellow. When you have finished knitting the body and sleeves, the only finishing required besides weaving in loose ends will be setting in the sleeves and sewing the sleeve seams.

SUPPLIES

50 gm skein baby or fingering weight yarn in three colors for the sweater and cap (50 gm is needed of the main color for the largest size, and less of the other colors.)

Circular knitting needles, size 3 and 1, or size needed for gauge (Size 16" or 24" are recommended. You will be knitting back and forth so use the length that is comfortable for you.)

3 (4, 5, 5) buttons, size ½"

Bobbin or piece of cardboard

Gauge: 7-8 st = 1"

CHECKERBOARD CARDIGAN

(DESIGNED BY CECI RIEHL)

BODY

Using smaller needle and **red yarn**, CO 84 (92, 100, 100) st. Work 1 row in k1, p1 rib.

Row 2: Change to **yellow**, *(cut red yarn)* work 1 row with yellow in k1, p1 rib.

Row 3: Buttonhole row: With yellow, k1, p1, yo, k1, p1, pull the second st on the right needle over the first and drop it, k1. Tie on **blue**, work to within 5 st of end of row in rib pattern. Tie on a second strand of yellow. *Pull about 5 yards of yellow from the other end of the ball, wind it on a bobbin or piece of cardboard and use this yarn for the button band. Continue to use the other yellow for the buttonhole band on the other edge. Both bands will be worked in solid yellow.* With second yellow yarn k1,p1,k1,p1,k1.

Row 4: With yellow k1, p1, k1, p1, k1; Tie on **red**, work across to other band continuing the k1, p1 rib. Work the 5 sts of the band with yellow k1, p1, k1, p1, k1.

From here on sweater is worked in stockinette st for the body and seed st. for the bands. The 5 sts in the band are the same on both inside and outside of the sweater. The bands continue in yellow seed st. all the way to the neck edge.

Row 5: With yellow work band in seed st. With the same **yellow** yarn, knit across **increasing 18 (18, 22, 22)** st evenly spaced across the 74 (82, 90, 90) red sts. Make the increases (m1) in every 4th st in the purl sts of the row below, starting with the (2nd, 6th, 2nd, 2nd) purl st. **102 (110, 122, 122 st)**. *Check this number accurately.* Work the band in **seed** st. with yellow.

(Note: All the color changes will be made between the yellow band and the body of the sweater. When changing colors, always cross the new color over the old one and hold the old one snugly in the other hand until you have worked a few sts. Then drop it but don't cut it until the directions say to.)

Row 6: Work band in yellow seed st; pick up **blue** from below. Purl across to other band. *Cut the longer yellow from the other side and tie it on this side.* Work band in yellow.

Row 7: Work band in yellow; pick up **red** from below; knit across; work band in yellow.

Row 8: Work band in yellow; purl across with **red** again *(2 rows of red here)*. Work band in yellow.

BANDS

Continue to work the bands in this manner. I will not continue to mention them. You will need to work 3, (4, 4, 5) buttonholes in the buttonhole band evenly spaced at about 1¾" (1⅜", 1½", 1¼") apart. The buttonholes will be on the right front as for a girl's sweater.

BEGIN CHECK PATTERN

Use the longer yellow yarn to work the buttonhole band and to work across the sweater, when yellow is called for in the pattern. Continue to use the shorter yellow yarn for the band on the other side. This will mean fewer ends to cut and weave in. When changing from one yellow to the other, always cross them in back as when changing colors.

● Red
○ Blue
☐ Yellow

Work 12 rows of check pattern on the 92 (100, 112, 112) sts between the yellow bands. Cut blue yarn. *The rest of the body is worked in red with yellow bands.* Continue in red and yellow until sweater measures 2¼" (2½", 3", 3½") from beginning. End with a purl row.

DIVIDE FOR ARMHOLES
RIGHT FRONT

Work 5 sts of band; knit 23 (25, 28, 28) st. Turn.

Work these 28 (30, 33, 33) sts as before, while at the same time working buttonholes in the buttonhole band. You will have a total of 2 (3, 3, 4) buttonholes in this section with the last one about 2" (3", 3¼", 4") up from the bottom edge. *(One more buttonhole will be worked in the neck band.)* Work until front measures 3¾" (4½", 5", 5¾"). End with a knit row.

SHAPE NECK OPENING

Next row: Work to last 8 sts (3 red, 5 yellow); W & T, leaving these 8 sts on needle.

Next row: Work to armhole.

Next row: Work to 2 sts before turn; W & T.

Repeat these two rows until 12 (13, 15, 15) sts remain in right front section. Cut yarn.

BACK

Tie yarn on at armhole. Knit across 46 (50, 56, 56) sts. Turn. Work these 46 (50, 56, 56) sts in stockinette st until back measures 5¼" (5½", 6", 6¾"). End with a purl row.

Bind off and join shoulder 12 (13, 15, 15) sts. Cut yarn. Transfer remaining front sts to smaller needle.

LEFT FRONT

Tie yarn on at left armhole. Work across in established pattern to center front. Work this side until it is the same length as the other front at center front. End with a purl row.

Next row: Work to last 8 sts. W & T.

Next row: Work back to armhole.

Next row: Work to 2 sts before turn; W & T.

Repeat these 2 rows until 12 (13, 15, 15) sts remain in front section. Stop at armhole edge. Do not cut yarn.

Using the same yarn, bind off and join these 12 (13, 15, 15) shoulder sts. Do not cut yarn. Knit across the remaining 11 (12, 13, 13) red sts of the left front section; work band in seed st with yellow yarn.

NECK BAND

(Note: The yellow buttonhole bands will continue to the neck edge.)

Work band in yellow seed st. Work buttonhole in buttonhole band. Work across the red sts in k1, p1, rib. Work right band in seed st. with yellow. Work 3 more rows in this manner. Bind off all sts with the appropriate color yarn. Cut and tie off loose ends.

SLEEVES

With red yarn, CO 26 (30, 36, 36). Knit 1 row in k1p1 rib. Add yellow yarn, but do not cut red. With yellow, work one row in k1p1 rib. Without cutting yellow, tie on blue. Work 1 row with blue in k1p1 rib. Work one more row in rib with red.

Continue to alternate the three colors yellow-blue-red for the rest of the sleeve, which will be worked in stockinette st.

Row 1: Knit with yellow.

Row 2: Purl with blue.

Row 3: Knit with red, increasing 1 st each edge.

Row 4: Purl with yellow.

Row 5: Knit with blue.

Row 6: Purl with red.

Repeat these 6 rows until sleeve reaches desired length: 4" (4½", 5", 5¾"), and at the same time, when sleeve width equals twice the armhole depth, stop increasing. End with a red row. Cut blue and yellow yarns. Work one more row in red. Bind off all sts.

FINISHING

Sew sleeves into armholes. Sew underarm sleeve seams, matching stripes. Press and block sweater following procedures recommended for your yarn. Sew buttons on button band corresponding to buttonholes.

SUPPLIES

⅓ yd. (⅓ yd., ½ yd., ½ yd.) cotton twill fabric to match the sweater

8" (11", 14", 17") elastic, ⅜" wide

CUTTING INSTRUCTIONS

From the cotton twill fabric, cut:

•Four pants (Pattern 26).

1 With right sides together, sew the side seams and the center front and back seams.

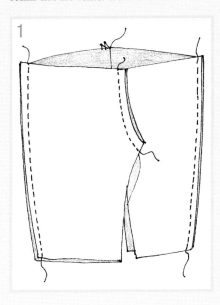

2 Press the lower edge of the pants ¼" to the wrong side and stitch.

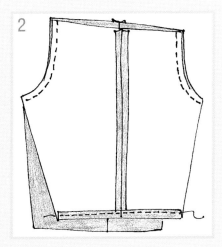

3 Serge or zigzag stitch the top edge of the pants. Press the top edge of the pants ¾" to the wrong side. Stitch ½" from the folded edge to form a casing, leaving a 1" opening in the back. Thread the elastic through the casing and secure the ends. Stitch the opening closed.

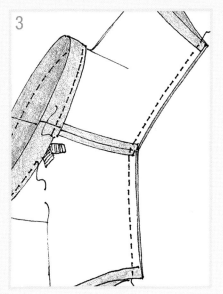

4 Sew the inner leg seam.

CO 60 (70, 80, 90) sts with red

Work as for sleeve for 1" (1", 1½", 1½").

BEGIN DECREASE ROWS

All knit rows: k1, ssk, knit across to last 3 st, k2tog, k1.

All purl rows: purl across.

Continue until 4 sts remain. Cut the working yarn, leaving an 18" tail. Cut the other yarns. Weave the 18" tail through the last 4 st on the needle and use this yarn to sew the seam down the back of the cap. Sew pompom to the tip.

Party Favor

BITTY TWIN BY PLEASANT COMPANY AND ADORA DOLL

Special occasions for baby dolls, such as a first birthday and a first Christmas require extra special outfits. The dresses and pinafores shown here have been designed to commemorate these events with customized embroidery. The fabric for each dress was chosen to symbolize each occasion: angels for Christmas and party balloons for a birthday. Each dress has been made using fast and easy construction techniques. The pinafores are "patternless" because each one is made by a square bib, long straps and a rectangular gathered skirt. The fun part comes with the embroidery! The pinafore bibs have been embroidered with a birthday cake, balloons and a sweet angel to symbolize their respective events. The skirt is decorated with phrases that can be programmed into your sewing machine to repeat along the hemline to say "Baby's First Christmas," or "Baby's First Birthday."

BABY'S FIRST BIRTHDAY DRESS AND PATTERNLESS PINAFORE

(DESIGNED BY MARILEE SAGAT)

SUPPLIES

⅓ yd. (½ yd., ⅔ yd. ⅔ yd.) cotton print fabric

⅓ yd. (⅓ yd., ½ yd., ½ yd.) white broadcloth

6" (7½", 8", 8") elastic, ⅛" wide

½ yd. (⅔ yd., ⅔ yd., ⅔ yd.) pre-gathered eyelet lace edging, ⅞" wide

Birthday cake embroidery design*

40 wt embroidery thread

Tear-away stabilizer

1" x 45" piece of iron-on interfacing

2" (3", 4", 4") Velcro strip for the dress

2" Velcro strip for the pinafore

*Used in this project: "Me and My Doll Clothes" by Joan Hinds for VSM Sewing, Inc.

CUTTING INSTRUCTIONS

From the cotton print fabric, cut:
- Two bodice fronts (Pattern 16).
- Four bodice backs (Pattern 17).
- Two sleeves (Pattern 8).
- One 5¾" x 36" (6¾" x 45", 7" x 45", 7½" x 45") skirt.

From the white broadcloth, cut:
- One 5" x 36" (6" x 40", 6¼" x 45", 6½" x 45") skirt.
- Four 1½" x 7¼" (1½" x 10", 1½" x 10½", 1¾" x 11") straps.
- One 1½" x 11¼" (15", 16½", 18") waistband.
- *Note:* Leave enough fabric to fit your embroidery embroidery hoop—at least enough to draw a rectangle 2¼" x 4" (2¾" x 5", 3½" x 5", 4" x 6").

BABY'S FIRST BIRTHDAY DRESS

BABY'S FIRST BIRTHDAY

1 With one front and two backs, sew the shoulder seams with right sides together. Press the seam allowances open. Repeat with the remaining front and backs for the lining.

2 With right sides together, sew the bodice and lining up one center back, around the neckline, and down the other center back edge. Clip the curves; trim the seam allowances and turn to the right side. Press.

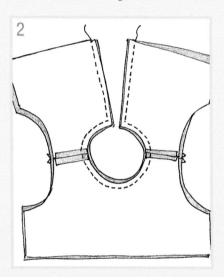

3 Baste around the armholes.

4 Narrow-hem the bottom of each sleeve edge. Cut the sleeve elastic in half. Starting at one side of the sleeve and ½" from the hemmed edge, sew the sleeve elastic by zigzag stitching over the top, stretching the elastic to the other side of the sleeve. Do not catch the elastic in your stitching except to secure the ends at each side. Gather the sleeve caps between the dots marked on the pattern piece.

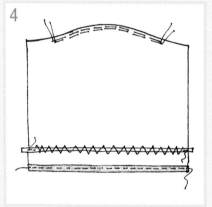

5 With right sides together, sew the sleeve caps to the armholes. Sew the underarm seam.

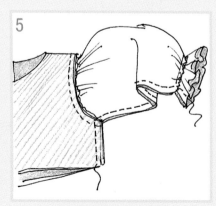

6 Press the two short ends of the skirt ¼" to the wrong side and stitch. Press one long edge ¼" to the wrong side, press another ¾" and stitch.

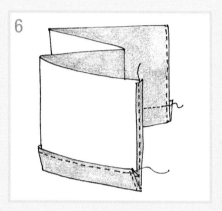

7 Gather the top edge of the skirt and stitch to the bodice with right sides together.

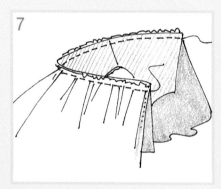

8 Lapping right over left, sew the Velcro to the back opening.

1 To embroider the birthday cake design, cut a piece of broadcloth to fit your embroidery hoop. Draw a rectangle 2¼" wide x 4" high (2¾" wide x 5" high, 3½" x 5" high, 4" wide x 6 high") for the bib on your fabric. Position the fabric in your hoop with the stabilizer so the short sides of the rectangle are at the top and bottom. Mark the center of each long edge (this will be the fold line). Embroider the design in the lower half of the pinafore bib. Remove from the hoop and tear away the stabilizer. Cut out the bib and fold it in half along the fold line with wrong sides together and press.

2 Sew a broadcloth strap to each side of the bib front by sandwiching the bib between two straps, as shown below.

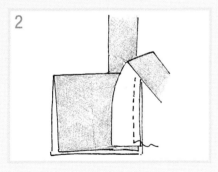

3 Open out the straps to the right side and press.

4 Cut the eyelet edging in half widthwise. Stitch the eyelet edging to the cut edges of the straps just beyond the heading of the eyelet. Cut away the heading and serge or zigzag stitch the edge to finish. Press the seam allowance to the wrong side and top stitch. Repeat with the remaining straps on the other side of the bib.

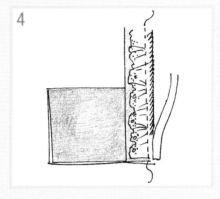

5 To embroider the skirt, serge or zigzag stitch one long edge of the skirt. Press the strip of interfacing to the wrong side of this edge. Press this edge 1" to the wrong side. Program your machine to say "Baby's First Birthday" and stitch along the pressed hem ¾" from the edge.

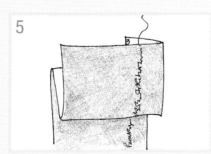

6 Press the short ends of the skirt ¼" to the wrong side and stitch. Gather the top edge of the skirt to fit the waistband. Press one long edge of the waistband ¼" to the wrong side. With the right side of the waistband to the wrong side of the skirt, sew the unpressed edge of the waistband to the gathered edge of the skirt, extending the short ends of the waistband ¼". Fold the waistband over to the right side of the skirt and topstitch, tucking in the short ends.

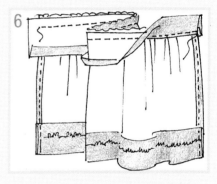

7 Serge or zigzag stitch the bottom edge of the pinafore bib and straps. Center the bib on the pinafore skirt with the bottom of the bib extending approximately ¼" beyond the bottom edge of the waistband and topstitch it in place.

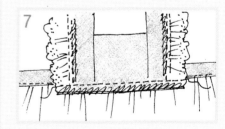

8 Cut the pinafore Velcro strip in half lengthwise. Cut each half in half again widthwise. Sew one part of the Velcro to each end of the pinafore skirt, lapping right over left. Sew the hook part of the Velcro to the right side of the end of each strap. Sew the loop half to the wrong side of the waistband 1" from each end.

BABY'S FIRST CHRISTMAS DRESS AND PATTERNLESS PINAFORE

(DESIGNED BY MARILEE SAGAT)

For both the dress and pinafore, follow the instructions for the Baby's First Birthday Dress and Pinafore on pages 94-95. Change the embroidered words on the pinafore to say "Baby's First Christmas" and embroider the angel design on the pinafore bib.

SUPPLIES

⅓ yd. (½ yd., ⅔ yd., ⅔ yd.) cotton print fabric

⅓ yd. (⅓ yd., ½ yd., ½ yd.) white broadcloth

6" (7½", 8", 8") elastic, ⅛" wide

½ yd. (⅔ yd., ⅔ yd., ⅔ yd.) pre-gathered eyelet lace edging, ⅞" wide

Angel embroidery design*

40 wt embroidery thread

Tear-away stabilizer

1" x 45" piece of iron-on interfacing

2" (3", 4", 4") Velcro strip for the dress

2" Velcro strip for the pinafore

*Used in this project: "Me and My Doll Clothes" by Joan Hinds for VSM Sewing, Inc.

CUTTING INSTRUCTIONS

From the cotton print fabric, cut:

- Two bodice fronts (Pattern 16).
- Four bodice backs (Pattern 17).
- Two sleeves (Pattern 8).
- One 5¾" x 36" (6¾" x 45", 7" x 45", 7½" x 45") skirt.

From the white broadcloth, cut:

- One 5" x 36" (6" x 40", 6¼" x 45", 6½" x 45") skirt.
- Four 1½" x 7¼" (1½" x 10", 1½" x 10½", 1¾" x 11") straps.
- One 1½" x 11¼" (15", 16½", 18") waistband.
- *Note:* Leave enough fabric to fit your embroidery hoop — at least enough to draw a rectangle 2¼" x 4" (2¾" x 5", 3½" x 5", 4" x 6").

Shining Star

The best present under the Christmas tree may be this baby doll all dressed up in her Holiday Star Dress. She is wearing a white dress that has a sheer overlay with gold stars. This fast and easy dress has puffed sleeves, a plain neckline and a gathered skirt. The sash, made from wire-edged gold ribbon, ties in the front. Topping off the outfit is the headband decorated with a gold lamé fabric star.

HEADBAND AND DRESS

SUPPLIES

⅓ yd. (½ yd., ⅔ yd., ⅔ yd.) white satin or taffeta fabric

⅓ yd. (½ yd., ⅔ yd., ⅔ yd.) sheer fabric with gold stars

8" (8", 11", 11") elastic for the sleeve, ⅛" wide

Scrap of gold lamé fabric

Scrap of heavy interfacing

10½" (12½", 13½", 14") elastic for the headband, ½" wide

2" (3", 4", 4") Velcro strip

⅔ yd. (1 yd., 1 yd., 1 yd.) gold wire edged ribbon, 1" wide

CUTTING INSTRUCTIONS

From the white satin or taffeta fabric, cut:
- Two dress fronts (Pattern 16).
- Four dress backs (Pattern 17).
- Two sleeves (Pattern 8).
- One 5½" x 36" (6¼" x 40", 6¾" x 45", 7¾" x 45") skirt.
- One 1½" x 17" (2" x 20", 2" x 25", 2" x 28") strip for the headband.

From the sheer fabric with gold stars, cut:
- One dress front (Pattern 16).
- Two dress backs (Pattern 17).
- Two sleeves (Pattern 8).
- One 5½" x 36" (6¼" x 40", 6¾" x 45", 7¾" x 45") skirt.

From the gold lamé fabric:
- *Note:* Leave room for two headband stars (Pattern 58). See Step 3.

HEADBAND

HEADBAND

1 Fold the white strip for the headband in half lengthwise and stitch. Turn it to the right side.

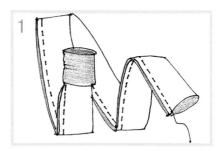

2 Thread the elastic through the headband and stitch to secure the ends. Sew the ends together.

3 For the star, first cut the scrap of gold lamé fabric in half. Trace the star pattern piece onto one piece of the gold lamé fabric. Place the piece of heavy interfacing underneath, followed by the other piece of lamé under both pieces. Using gold thread, stitch around the star with a zigzag stitch. Trim closely around the stitching.

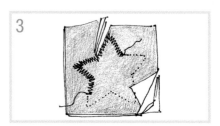

4 Tack the star to the front of the headband.

1 Place the sheer fabric front over one white front and two sheer back pieces over two white back pieces. Baste around the edges to secure. From now on, treat these pieces as one. With right sides together, sew the backs to the fronts at the shoulders. Repeat with the remaining white front and back pieces for the lining.

2 With right sides together, sew the bodice to its lining up each center back and around the neckline. Clip the curves; turn to the right side and press. Baste around the armholes.

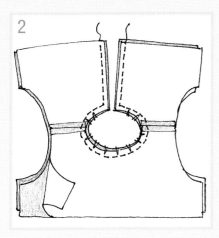

3 Place the sheer fabric sleeves over the white sleeves and baste around the edges. Press the lower sleeve edges ¼" to the wrong side and stitch.

4 Cut the elastic for the sleeve in half. Starting at one side of the sleeve and ½" from the hemmed edge, sew the sleeve elastic by zigzag stitching over the top, stretching the elastic to the other side of the sleeve. Do not catch the elastic in your stitching except to secure the ends at each side. Gather the sleeve caps between dots marked on the pattern piece.

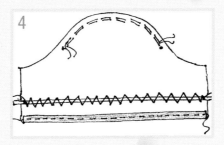

5 With right sides together, sew the sleeves to the armholes. Sew the underarm seam from the sleeve edge to the lower edge of the bodice.

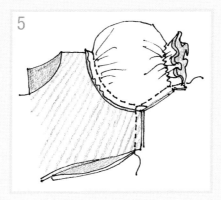

6 Press the short ends of each skirt piece ¼" to the wrong side and stitch. Press one long edge ¼" to the wrong side, press another ½" and stitch.

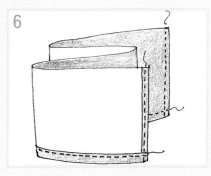

7 Place the wrong side of the sheer fabric skirt over the right side of the white skirt. Gather the top edges of the skirt together. With right sides together, sew the skirt to the bodice.

8 Lapping right over left, sew the Velcro to the back opening.

9 Tie the ribbon around the waist with the bow at the front. Cut off any excess, if desired.

Gingerbread Holiday

ADORA DOLLS

These dolls are enjoying gingerbread cookies in their matching twin outfits. Both the dress and the pants are sewn from fabric printed with hearts and gingerbread men. The boy looks especially dapper in his button-front shirt with bow tie and pants with suspenders. The girl's dress has a collar with a hand embroidery technique called shadow appliqué. This is done by placing brightly colored fabric shapes, such as a heart, over a base fabric. A sheer overlay is placed over the top with the shapes visible from underneath, but they now have a more subdued color. The shapes are outlined with a running stitch done with matching sewing thread.

BUTTON-DOWN SHIRT, BOW TIE AND PANTS

SUPPLIES

¼ yd. (⅓ yd., ½ yd., ½ yd.) gingerbread or other print cotton fabric

8" (11", 14", 17") elastic for the waist, ⅜" wide

2 heart buttons for the pants, ½" (½", ¾", ¾")

¼ yd. (¼ yd., ¼ yd., ⅓ yd.) cream cotton fabric

3 (4, 4, 4) buttons, size ¼"

3 (4, 4, 4) small snaps

Scrap of red print cotton fabric for the bow tie

5½" (7", 9", 9") elastic for the bow tie, ¼" wide

CUTTING INSTRUCTIONS

From the print cotton fabric, cut:
- Four pants (Pattern 26).
- Two straps 1½" x 7½" (2" x 10", 2½" x 11½", 2½" x 12½") for the pants.

From the cream cotton fabric, cut:
- Four shirt fronts (Pattern 44).
- Two shirt backs (Pattern 45).
- Two sleeves (Pattern 25).
- One collar (Pattern 47).

From the red print fabric, cut:
- One bow tie (Pattern 61).
- One bow tie center (Pattern 62).

1 With right sides together, sew two fronts to one back at the shoulder seams. Repeat with the other fronts and back to make a lining. Press the seam allowances open.

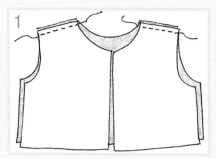

2 Fold the collar in half lengthwise with right sides together. Stitch across the short ends. Clip the corners; turn to the right side and press.

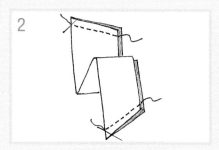

3 With right sides together, center the collar along the neckline of the shirt. Stitch. *Note:* The collar does not extend all the way to the center front edges.

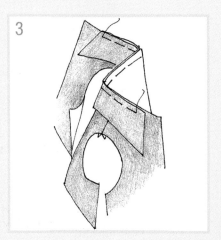

4 With right sides together, pin the shirt lining to the shirt, sandwiching the collar in between. Sew around the neckline, down the center fronts, and the bottom edges of both fronts and the back. Clip the curves; turn to the right side and press.

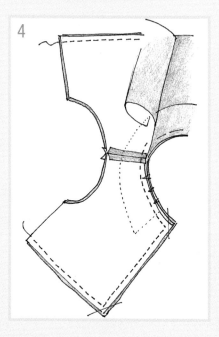

5 Baste the lining to the shirt around the armholes.

6 Serge or zigzag stitch the lower edge of the sleeves. Press the lower edge ¼" to the wrong side and stitch. Gather the sleeve caps between the dots.

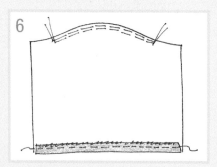

7 With right sides together, sew the sleeves to the armholes, easing in the sleeve. Sew the underarm seams from the cuff to the waist.

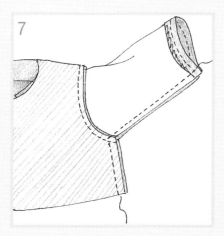

8 Lapping left over the right, sew the buttons to the left front as marked on the pattern piece.

9 Sew the snaps underneath the buttons.

ADORA DOLL

1 Fold the bow tie in half lengthwise with right sides together and stitch along the long edges. Turn to the right side and press. Fold it in thirds so the raw edges are in the back of the bow.

2 Press the long edges of the bow tie center ¼" to the wrong side. Wrap it around the center of the bow tie very tightly and stitch the ends together.

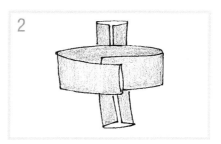

3 Stitch each end of the elastic to the back of the bow tie center.

4 Place the bow tie over the head of the doll. The elastic should go under the collar of the shirt.

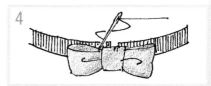

1 With right sides together, sew the side seams and the center front and back seams of the pants.

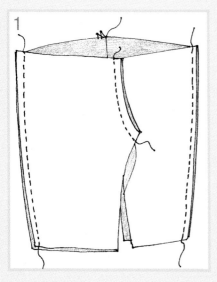

2 Press the lower edge of the pants ¼" to the wrong side and stitch.

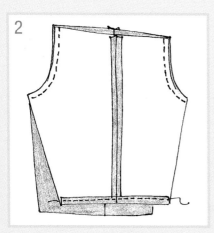

3 Serge or zigzag stitch the top edge of the pants. Press the top edge of the pants ¾" to the wrong side. Stitch ½" from the folded edge to form a casing, leaving a 1" opening in the back. Thread the elastic through the casing and secure the ends. Stitch the opening closed.

4 Sew the inner leg seam.

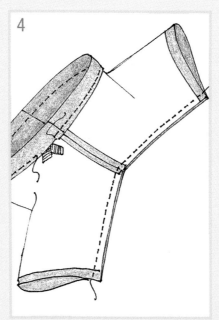

5 Fold the straps in half lengthwise with wrong sides together. Stitch along the long edges and one short end. Turn to the right side and press.

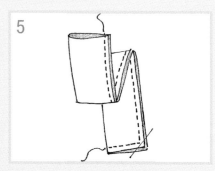

6 Pin the raw ends approximately ¼" below the waist at the inside back of the pants and ¾" (1", 1", 1") away from the center back seam. Topstitch over the previous waistline stitching. Bring the other end to the front, crossing the straps at the back, and tack to the outside of the waistband ¾" (1", 1", 1") away from the center front seam.

7 Sew a heart button to the top of each strap.

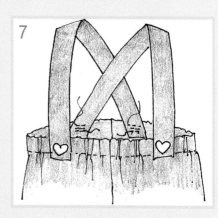

GINGERBREAD DRESS AND HEADBAND

SUPPLIES

½ yd. (½ yd., ⅔ yd., ⅔ yd.) gingerbread or other print cotton fabric

¼ yd cream fabric for the collar

¼ yd. white sheer cotton organdy or voile for the collar overlay

Scraps of red and brown fabric for the shadow appliqué shapes

Red and brown sewing thread to match the appliqué shapes

⅔ yd. pre-gathered eyelet lace edging for the collar, ⅞" (1¼", 1¼", 1½") wide

Skein each of red, brown and black embroidery floss

36" (40", 45", 45") pre-gathered eyelet lace edging for the skirt, 2" (2", 3", 3") wide

6" (7½", 8", 8") elastic, ⅛" wide

2" (3", 4", 4") Velcro strip

10½" (12½", 13½", 14") elastic for the headband, ½" wide

⅓ yd. satin ribbon for the bow on the headband, ⅝" (1", 1", 1") wide

CUTTING INSTRUCTIONS

From the print cotton fabric, cut:
• Two bodice fronts (Pattern 16).
• Four bodice backs (Pattern 17).
• Two sleeves (Pattern 8).
• One 6" x 36" (7¾" x 40", 8" x 45", 8½" x 45") skirt.
• One 1½" x 17" (2" x 20", 2" x 25", 2" x 28") strip for the headband.

From the cream fabric, cut:
• Two collar fronts (Pattern 59).
• Four collar backs (Pattern 60).

From the white sheer cotton organdy or voile, cut:
• One collar front (Pattern 59).
• Two collar backs (Pattern 60).

From the brown fabric, cut:
• Three gingerbread shapes (Pattern 63).

From the red fabric, cut:
• Two hearts (Pattern 63).

GINGERBREAD DRESS

1 With one front and two backs, sew the shoulder seams with right sides together. Press the seam allowances open. Repeat with the remaining front and backs for the lining.

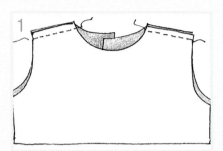

2 For the collar, use temporary spray adhesive to place the gingerbread and heart shapes on the cream front collar, as marked on the pattern piece. Pin the wrong side of the sheer front collar over the right side of the cream front collar.

3 Using one length of matching sewing thread, make small running stitches around each heart and gingerbread shape.

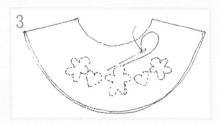

4 With one strand of black floss, make two eyes with French knots on the gingerbread men.

5 Make three buttons on each gingerbread man with French knots using one strand of red floss.

6 Pin the wrong side of the sheer collar backs over the right side of the collar backs. From now on, the collar fabrics will be treated as one.

7 With right sides together, sew the front collar to two backs along the shoulder seams. Repeat with the remaining pieces for the lining.

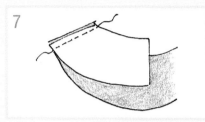

8 Sew the collar eyelet lace to the curved lower edge of the collar, stopping ¼" before the side edges and turning the raw ends ¼" to the wrong side. Cut off any excess.

9 Stitch the collars together along the lower curved edge. Clip the curves; turn to the right side and press.

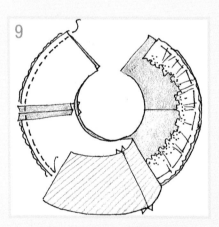

10 Fold the raw side edges ¼" to the wrong side and top stitch together.

11 Pin the finished collar to the neckline of the dress and baste. *Note:* The collar does not extend all the way to the center back opening.

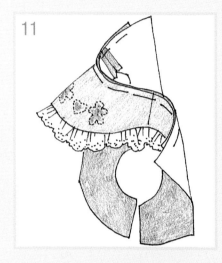

12 With right sides together, sew the bodice and its lining up one center back, around the neckline, and down the other center back edge. Clip the curves; trim the seam allowances and turn to the right side. Press.

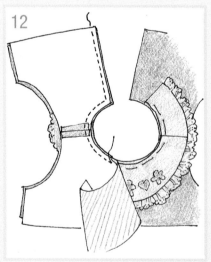

13 Baste around the armholes.

14 Narrow-hem the bottom of each sleeve edge. Cut the sleeve elastic in half. Starting at one side of the sleeve and ½" from the hemmed edge, sew the sleeve elastic by zigzag stitching over the top, stretching the elastic to the other side of the sleeve. Do not catch the elastic in your stitching except to secure the ends at each side. Gather the sleeve caps between the dots marked on the pattern piece.

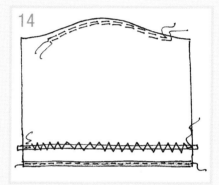

15 With right sides together, sew the sleeve caps to the armholes. Sew the underarm seam.

16 Press the short ends of the skirt ¼" to the wrong side and stitch.

17 Press the short ends of the skirt eyelet lace ¼" to the wrong side and stitch.

18 Pin the eyelet to one of the long edges of the skirt so the heading is ¼" from the stitching line. Stitch with a straight stitch and then cut off the heading. Serge or zigzag stitch this seam to finish.

19 Fold the hem 1" (1", 2", 2") to the wrong side and press. (The eyelet will hang below the skirt.) Stitch.

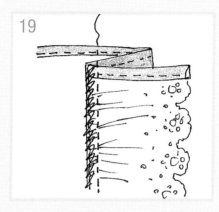

20 Gather the top edge of the skirt and stitch to the bodice with right sides together.

21 Lapping right over left, sew the Velcro to the back opening.

1 Fold the headband strip in half lengthwise with right sides together and stitch. Turn to the right side.

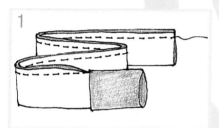

2 Thread the headband elastic through it and stitch at each end to secure. Sew the fabric ends together.

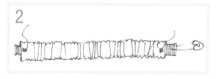

3 Tie a bow with the ribbon and tack it to the front of the center of the headband.

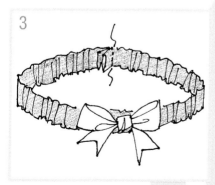

Christening Gown

LEE MIDDLETON

A special celebration gown and bonnet uses beautiful fabrics and laces, but does not have to be difficult to make. This gown is made with white cotton batiste or broadcloth and is trimmed with elegant rayon Venice lace. You can substitute any other lace if you prefer. For fine cotton laces, buy extra yardage. You can pull the thread in the lace heading to gather it for a less tailored look.

CHRISTENING GOWN AND BONNET

SUPPLIES

½ yd. (⅔ yd., ¾ yd., 1 yd.) white broadcloth

⅔ yd. (1 yd., 1 yd., 1 yd.) lace edging, ¾" wide

⅔ yd. (1 yd., 1 yd., 1 yd.) lace edging, 1¼" wide

1¼ yd. lace edging, 2" (3", 3", 3") wide

6" (7½", 8", 8") elastic, ⅛" wide

½ yd. satin ribbon for the back opening of the bonnet, ⅛" wide

⅔ yd. ribbon for the bonnet ties, ⅝" (⅞", ⅞", ⅞") wide

2" (3", 4", 4") Velcro strip

CUTTING INSTRUCTIONS

From the white broadcloth, cut:

• Two bodice fronts (Pattern 16).

• Four bodice backs (Pattern 17).

• Two sleeves (Pattern 8).

• One bonnet (Pattern 5).

• One 8" x 40" (13" x 45", 15" x 45", 17" x 45") skirt.

CHRISTENING GOWN

CHRISTENING GOWN

1 Cut two pieces of narrow edging to fit down the center of one of the fronts. Place them along the center front with the straight edges together. Zigzag stitch the straight edges.

2 Measure 1" from the center straight edges to both the right and the left. Cut two more pieces of narrow edging to fit along this measurement. Sew another row of lace edging along the straight edge.

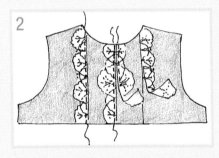

3 With one front and two backs, sew the shoulder seams with right sides together. Press the seam allowances open. Repeat with the remaining front and backs for the lining.

4 With right sides together, sew the bodice and its lining up one center back, around the neckline, and down the other center back edge. Clip the curves; trim the seam allowances and turn to the right side. Press.

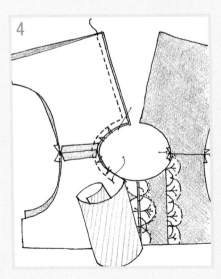

5 Baste around the armholes.

6 Press the lower edge of the sleeves ¼" to the wrong side. Cut two pieces of the narrow edging to fit the lower edge of the sleeves. Place the heading of the lace under the pressed edges and topstitch.

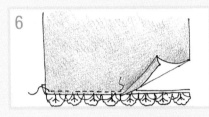

7 Cut the sleeve elastic in half. Starting at one side of the sleeve and ½" from the hemmed edge, sew the sleeve elastic by zigzag stitching over the top, stretching the elastic to the other side of the sleeve. Do not catch the elastic in your stitching except to secure the ends at each side. Gather the sleeve caps between the dots marked on the pattern piece.

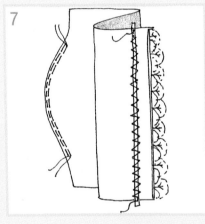

8 With right sides together, sew the sleeve caps to the armholes. Sew the underarm seam.

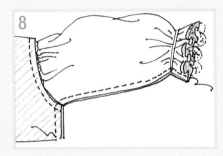

9 Press the short sides of the skirt ¼" to the wrong side and stitch. Press one of the long edges of the skirt ¼" to the wrong side. Place the heading of the wide lace edging under the pressed edge and topstitch, folding the raw ends of the lace ¼" to the wrong side.

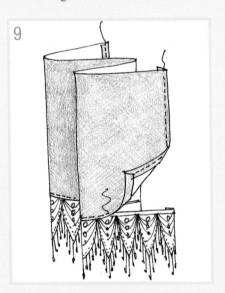

10 Gather the remaining long edge to fit the bodice. With right sides together, sew the bodice to the skirt.

11 Turn one end of the medium-width lace ¼" to the wrong side. Pin the end to the back bodice just above the skirt/bodice seam line and ½" away from the sleeve seam, as marked on the pattern piece. With a narrow zigzag stitch, sew the heading of this lace up the back bodice, over the shoulder, and down the front bodice. When you reach the skirt/bodice seam, miter the corner, and stitch across the front of the bodice just above the seam. Miter the corner and stitch up over the shoulder as done on the other side. Cut off the lace at the skirt/bodice seam and turn the end under before you finish the stitching.

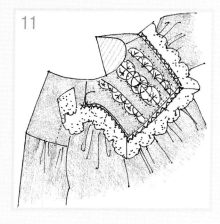

12 Lapping right over left, sew the Velcro to the back opening.

1 Press the sides of the bonnet ¼" to the wrong side. Press another ¼" and stitch.

2 Press the long curved edge of the bonnet ¼" to the wrong side. Fold another ½" and stitch to form a casing.

3 Press the front opening edge ¼" to the wrong side. Place the heading of the remaining medium-width lace under the folded edge and topstitch.

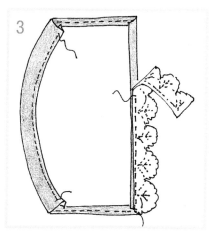

4 Cut the wider ribbon in half. Fold one edge on each piece ½" to the wrong side and stitch at an angle to the side front edges.

5 Thread the ⅛" ribbon through the casing and stitch the ribbon at the center of the casing to secure. Try the bonnet on the baby doll and tie the ribbon at the back of the head.

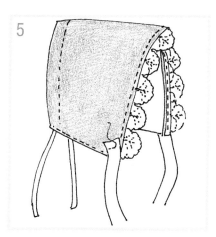

Baby Doll Essentials

No baby doll's wardrobe would be complete without quilts, blankets and other essential items. They are such fun to make with all the adorable prints found in flannel and fleece today. The motifs in the print can actually help you decide on a theme for your project. The quilts shown here are basic patchwork squares that feature appliqué on the large quilt and machine embroidery on the smaller quilt. The knitted blanket also is made with brightly colored yarn squares with a scalloped edge.

Fleece is a great fabric to use for doll blankets. The Butterfly Appliqué Blanket uses appliqués made from solid color fleece that are stitched only on the center. The other fleece blanket has embroidery on a solid color fleece "patch" that is then appliquéd on the blanket. Blanket edges can be finished simply by using a scalloped rotary cutter, or by serging the edge with the wide variety of decorative threads available today.

Soft, cuddly flannel is a timeless fabric used in doll blankets. One easy method to decorate a flannel blanket is to hem the edge of the blanket with an interesting machine decorative stitch. Stitched to the corner can be an embroidered appliqué chosen from one of the many baby embroidery designs available. Two layers of flannel can be used to make another warm blanket. One of the pieces is larger than the other and is folded over to the front with mitered corners. A special celebration blanket can be made from double-faced quilted flannel with a satin binding. A customized embroidery design with the doll's name (or just "baby") can be stitched in one corner.

SUPPLIES

½ yd. heart print flannel

½ yd. coordinating print flannel with a motif, such as butterflies

1⅔ yd. pink swirl print flannel

¼ yd. blue swirl print flannel

¼ yd. green flannel

¼ yd. yellow flannel for the binding

Package of yellow chenille-by-the-yard strips

Fusible web

1 yd. white flannel for the lining

CUTTING INSTRUCTIONS

From the heart print flannel, cut:
- Eight 4½" squares.
- Four 1" x 32" binding strips.

From the coordinating print flannel with a motif, cut:
- Eight 4½" squares, centering the square over the motif.

From the pink swirl print flannel, cut:
- Two 2" x 21" strips.
- Two 4½" x 32" border strips.
- Two 4½" x 24¼" border strips.
- One 31½" square for the backing.
- *Note:* Leave room for four hearts (Pattern 76). See Step 1.

From the blue swirl flannel, cut:
- Three 2" x 21" strips.
- Two 2" x 24¼" strips.
- *Note:* Leave room for four hearts (Pattern 76). See Step 1.

From the green flannel, cut:
- 12 strips 2" x 4½".

From chenille-by-the-yard, cut:
- Eight lengths 10"-11".

From the yellow flannel, cut:
- Four 1½" x 32" binding strips.

From the white flannel, cut:
- One 31½" square for the lining.

1 Trace four hearts using the heart pattern onto a piece of fusible web. Iron the web to the wrong side of a piece of pink swirl fabric, following the manufacturer's instructions. Repeat with the blue swirl flannel. Cut out the hearts, peel off the paper backing and iron each one to the center of the heart print flannel squares.

2 Make a long pieced strip using the heart and motif squares with the green strips. Begin with a pink heart square and stitch it to the long side of the green strip. Sew the other side of the green strip to a motif square. Continue sewing a green strip, followed by a blue heart square, green strip and a motif square.

3 Make a second pieced strip with the same pieces, beginning with a motif square stitched to a green strip, followed by a blue heart square, green strip, motif square, green strip and a pink heart square.

4 Make a third pieced strip, beginning with a blue heart square stitched to a green strip, followed by a motif square, green strip, pink heart square, green strip and a motif square.

5 Make a fourth pieced strip, beginning with a motif square stitched to a green strip, followed by a pink heart square, green strip, motif square and a blue heart square. Press all seam allowances open.

6 Using the chenille-by-the-yard strips and beginning at the point, stitch down the center of each strip to the outside edges of the hearts. Spritz the chenille strips with water and brush with a stiff brush to create the chenille. Let dry.

7 With right sides together, sew the right edge of the first long pieced strip to a 21" piece of pink swirl flannel and the left edge of the first long pieced strip to a 21" strip of blue swirl flannel.

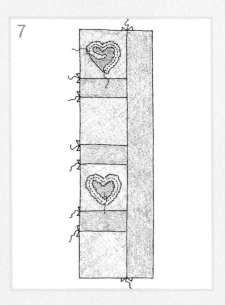

8 Sew the other edge of the pink strip to the second pieced strip.

9 Sew the other edge of the pieced strip to the 21" strip of blue swirl flannel.

10 Stitch the other edge of the blue strip to the third pieced strip.

11 Sew the other edge of the third pieced strip to the 21" strip of pink flannel.

12 Sew the other edge of the pink flannel strip to the fourth long pieced strip.

13 Sew the other edge of the fourth pieced strip to a 21" strip of the blue swirl flannel. The hearts should be in alternating squares.

14 Press all of the seam allowances open.

15 Sew the remaining two 24½" blue swirl flannel strips to the top and bottom edges of the pieced strips.

16 With right sides together, sew the 24¼" pink swirl flannel strips to the sides of the quilt. Sew the 32" pink swirl flannel strips to the top and bottom of the quilt. Press the seam allowances open.

17 Place the white lining flannel under the quilt top. Place the pink swirl flannel quilt back under the quilt top and lining so the wrong sides are together. Baste in place around the edges.

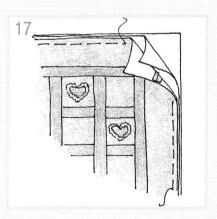

18 Press the four 32" heart print flannel binding strips in half lengthwise with wrong sides together. Press one long edge of the 32" yellow binding strips ¼" to the wrong side. Sew the unpressed edge of one of the yellow strips to one side on the back of the quilt with right sides together. Fold the edge over to the right side and stitch, placing a folded heart strip under the pressed edge so approximately ¼" extends out beyond the folded edge. Repeat with the other side of the quilt.

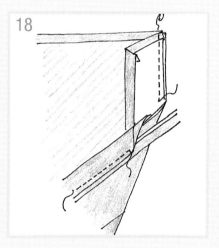

19 Sew the remaining two yellow and heart print strips to the top and the bottom of the quilt, turning the short ends of the yellow strip under ¼" after folding it over to the right side.

20 Stitch in the ditch along the quilt squares, if desired.

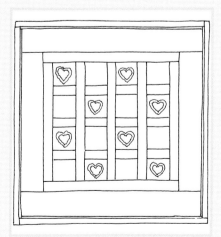

EMBROIDERED SQUARES QUILT

SUPPLIES

½ yd. white cotton fabric

½ yd. print cotton fabric with a motif, such as teddy bears

½ yd. pink gingham fabric

¼ yd. yellow print cotton fabric

1½ yd. teal stripe cotton fabric

1 yd. white flannel for the lining

5 machine embroidery designs*

40 wt. embroidery thread

Tear-away stabilizer

*Used in this project: "Just for Baby, Just for Baby II and Teddy Bears II" by Designs So Fine, Inc.

CUTTING INSTRUCTIONS

From the white cotton fabric, cut:
- •Five pieces large enough to fit in your embroidery hoop (to trim down to 4½" square later).

•From the print cotton fabric with a motif, cut:
Four 4½" squares, centering the square over the motif.
Four 1" x 26½" border strips.

•From the pink gingham fabric, cut:
Two 2" x 15½" strips.
Two 2" x 18½" strips.
Four 2" x 27" binding strips.

•From the yellow print fabric, cut:
Six 4½" x 2" strips.

•From the teal stripe fabric, cut:
Two 2" x 15½" strips.
Two 4½" x 18½" border strips.
Two 4½" x 26½" border strips.
One 26½" square for the backing.

•From the white flannel, cut:
One 26½" square for the lining.

1 Embroider one design on each white cotton fabric piece according to your machine's instructions. Tear away the stabilizer. Trim the pieces to 4½" squares, centering the designs.

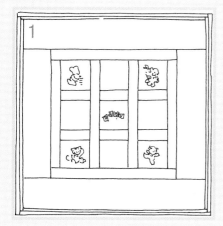

2 Make a long pieced strip using the embroidered and motif squares with the short yellow print strips. Begin with an embroidered square and stitch it to the long side of the yellow strip. Sew the other side of the yellow strip to a motif square. Continue sewing a yellow strip, followed by an embroidered square.

3 Make a second pieced strip with the same pieces, beginning with a motif square stitched to a yellow strip, followed by an embroidered square, yellow strip and a motif square.

4 Make a third pieced strip just like the first one. Press all seam allowances open.

5 With right sides together, sew the right edge of the first pieced strip to the 15½" teal strip and the left edge of the first pieced strip to a 15½" gingham strip.

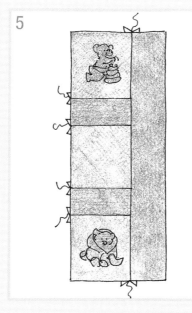

6 Sew the other side of the teal strip to the second pieced strip.

7 Sew the other side of the pieced strip to the second 15½" teal stripe strip.

8 Stitch the other side of the teal stripe to the third pieced strip.

9 Sew the remaining 15½" gingham strip to the right edge of the third pieced strip.

10 Press all of the seam allowances open.

11 Sew the remaining pink gingham strips to the top and the bottom edges of the pieced strips.

12 Sew the 18½" teal stripe strips to each side of the quilt.

13 Sew the 26½" teal strips to the top and bottom edges of the quilt. Press all seam allowances open.

14 Place the lining flannel under the quilt top. Place the quilt back under the quilt top and lining with wrong sides together. Baste in place around the edges.

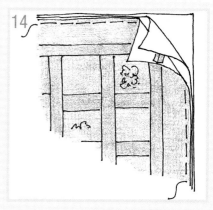

15 Press the 26½" print border strips in half lengthwise with wrong sides together. Baste the cut edges along the sides of the quilt top, overlapping the edges.

16 Fold the 27" pink gingham binding strips in half lengthwise with wrong sides together and press. With right sides together, sew the cut edges of one of the binding strips to the back of the quilt along each side. Fold the binding to the front of the quilt and top stitch close to the folded edges. Repeat with the top and bottom edges of the quilt, tucking in the short ends of the binding before top stitching.

17 Stitch in the ditch along the quilt squares, if desired.

KNITTED BLANKET

KNITTED BLANKET

(DESIGNED BY CECI RIEHL)

This blanket has several options. It can be made in squares of five colors—or four solid colors and one multi-color yarn, as shown in the photos. The blanket in the photo consists of 25 squares. Refer to the diagrams at right for a larger blanket of 49 squares. You may make the blanket larger by using a larger yarn and needle. Likewise, using a smaller yarn and needle will result in a smaller blanket.

BLANKET SIZES

A 25-square blanket made of 5" squares will be about 26" square. A 49-square blanket of 5" squares will be about 36" square. After you've made one square, you can use simple math to calculate the finished size of the blanket based on the measurement of your square.

The blanket in the photo above was made of sport-weight yarn and knitted on a #4 needle.

You will also find options for random placement of the colored squares, or a symmetric design—or make up your own design using graph paper and colored pencils.

Your next choice is whether to do the blanket in one piece or in strips that will be sewn together.

MAKE A GAUGE SWATCH

Cast on 24 st. Knit 38 rows. Cast off. Lay this square on a flat surface and check to see that it is square. If not adjust the number of rows needed to produce a square. It must be an even number. Cast off. Use that number for all the squares.

INSTRUCTIONS TO KNIT THE BLANKET IN STRIPS

Cast on 24 st with the blue yarn. Knit 38 rows (or number needed to achieve a square) Change to multi yarn. Knit the same number of rows. Change to pink yarn. Knit the same number of rows. Continue in this manner, following the color charts. When this strip is done (after 5 or 7 squares have been completed), bind off all sts. Work the next strip in the same way. When all strips are completed, sew them together, matching up corners as you assemble the blanket. Refer to the diagram to get the strips in the right order.

Pattern for color placement of squares. For the larger blanket, make all 49 squares; for the smaller blanket, work the 25 squares in the lower right-hand corner.

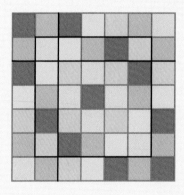

Color diagram for symmetric design. For the smaller blanket, use the 25 squares in the center of diagram.

CROCHET STITCH ABBREVIATIONS

Sl 1: Slip 1

Sc: Single crochet

Dc: Double crochet

Tc: Triple crochet

SCALLOPED EDGING

Chose any color yarn for the edging.

INSTRUCTIONS TO KNIT THE BLANKET IN ONE PIECE

(Use the color charts for color placement.)

Using the color you will use for the edging, cast on (120 st. for 25-square blanket or 168 st. for 49-square blanket) using a 36" to 40" circular needle.

Knit one row.

Next row: Knit 24, tie on next color, knit 24; tie on next color, knit 24;

Continue in this manner, following the color chart.

Note: Start at the bottom either at the right or left side. It doesn't matter since the blanket will be reversible. Just be consistent.

Knit the first row of blocks. They should be 38 rows or any even number of rows needed to make squares. Cut all yarns leaving 6" tails to weave in later.

Next row: Tie on new colors for each block again according to the color chart. Continue in this manner until all the squares have been completed. Knit one more row with the edging color. Bind off all sts. Weave in cut ends.

FINISHING (FOR BLANKET KNITTED IN ONE PIECE)

Using edge color, crochet one row single crochet across each side of the blanket, working 24 sts across each square.

SCALLOPED EDGING

(For all sizes and methods of construction.)

Start 3 st before a corner.

Work sc, dc, 3 tc in corner st, dc, sc, sl 1. (sc, dc, tc, dc, sc, sl 1).

Repeat the sts in parentheses across to the next corner.

Try to work 4 scallops across each square to make the corners work out so that the triple crochet is in a corner stitch.

Work 3 tc in the corner stitch.

Work around the blanket.

Sl 1 in first sc to join.

Cut yarn.

Weave in ends.

CELEBRATION BLANKET

CELEBRATION BLANKET

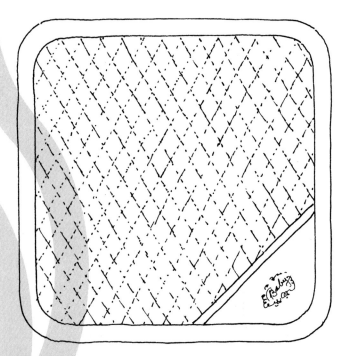

SUPPLIES

1 yd. white double-faced quilted flannel

15" square of white cotton fabric

⅔ yd. white decorative braid, ⅜" wide

"Baby" embroidery design*

40 wt. decorative thread

Tear away stabilizer

2 yd. white satin bias strip, 5" wide

Round dinner plate

*Used in this project: "Baby and Hearts" by VSM Sewing, Inc.

CUTTING INSTRUCTIONS

From the white double-faced quilted flannel, cut:
 •One 30" square.

1 Round the corners of the 30" white flannel square using a dinner plate as a guide.

2 Place the white cotton fabric over one corner of the blanket. Cut around the corner to match the flannel. Measure 12" from the corner along the two sides and draw a diagonal line connecting the two points. Cut the white cotton fabric along this line.

3 Embroider the design in the center of this white cotton piece with stabilizer. Be sure to place the design diagonally on the fabric. Remove the stabilizer.

4 Pin the embroidered fabric over a corner of the quilt. Baste all the edges.

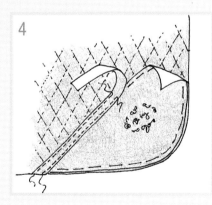

5 Place the braid over the diagonal edge and topstitch along both sides.

6 Press the bias binding in half lengthwise with wrong sides together. Press the cut ends at the beginning of the binding ½" to the wrong side. Sew the cut edges of the binding to the wrong side of the blanket with a ½" seam allowance. Cut off the excess. Fold the binding over to the right side and press. (Note the binding will be much wider on the right side.) Stitch.

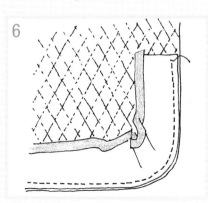

BUTTERLY FLEECE BLANKET

BUTTERFLY FLEECE BLANKE

1 Arrange the butterflies on one corner of the 27" square, as shown in the photo.

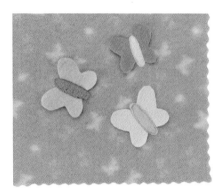

2 Place the pink body over the teal butterfly and stitch around the outside edge of the body to secure the butterfly to the blanket.

3 Place the teal body over the yellow butterfly and stitch as with the previous butterfly.

4 Place the yellow body over the pink butterfly and stitch as with the previous butterflies.

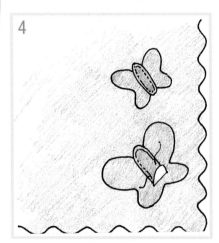

SUPPLIES

¾ yd. print or solid fleece

Scraps of yellow, pink and teal fleece for the butterflies

CUTTING INSTRUCTIONS

From the print or solid fleece, cut:
* One 27" square, using a wavy blade rotary cutter.

From the yellow fleece, cut:
* One large butterfly (Pattern 74).
* One small butterfly body (Pattern 73).

From the pink fleece, cut:
* One large butterfly body (Pattern 75).
* One small butterfly (Pattern 72).

From the teal fleece, cut:
* One large butterfly (Pattern 74).
* One large butterfly body (Pattern 75).

APPLIQUÉ FLEECE BLANKET

APPLIQUÉ FLEECE BLANKET

1 Round the corners of the 32" fleece square using a small plate as a guide.

2 Embroider the designs onto the mint green and pink fleece. Tear away the stabilizer.

3 Measure ¾" from the embroidery designs on all four sides and draw these lines on the back of the embroidered patches. Cut them along these lines with a pinking shears.

4 Spray the backs of the embroidered patches with temporary spray adhesive and place them on one corner, overlapping the edges, as shown in the photo. Stitch ¼" from the pinked edges.

5 Using the heavyweight embroidery thread in the upper and lower loopers of your serger and matching sewing thread in the needle, stitch along the edge of the blanket.

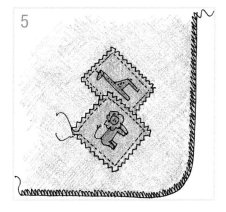

SUPPLIES

1 yd. print or solid color fleece

Scrap of mint green fleece, large enough to fit in a machine embroidery hoop

Scrap of pink fleece, large enough to fit in a machine embroidery hoop

Lion and giraffe machine embroidery designs*

40 wt. embroidery thread

Tear-away stabilizer

2 spools heavyweight embroidery thread for the blanket edging

Pinking shears

Temporary spray adhesive

Small round plate

*Used in this project: "Sweet Lullaby" by Deb Strain for VSM Sewing, Inc.

CUTTING INSTRUCTIONS

From the print or solid color fleece, cut:

• One 32" square.

APPLIQUÉ FLANNEL BLANKET

APPLIQUE FLANNEL BLANKE

SUPPLIES

1 yd. print flannel

Scrap of blue flannel

Baby rattle machine embroidery design*

40 wt. embroidery thread

Tear-away stabilizer

Pinking shears

Temporary spray adhesive

*Used in this project: "Baby II" by Amazing Designs

CUTTING INSTRUCTIONS

From the print flannel, cut:
- •One 32" square.

1 Press the edges of the 32" square ½" to the wrong side, mitering the corners.

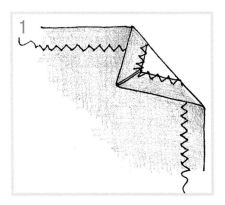

2 Using machine embroidery thread, stitch along the folded edge ½" from the fold with a decorative stitch, catching the raw edge underneath.

3 Place the blue flannel in the hoop with the stabilizer and embroider the design. Remove from the hoop and tear away the stabilizer.

4 Measure 1" from the embroidery design on all four sides and draw these lines on the back of the embroidered patch. Cut along these lines with a pinking shears.

5 Using temporary spray adhesive, spray the back of the patch and place in one of the corners of the blanket. Stitch with decorative thread ¼" from the pinked edge.

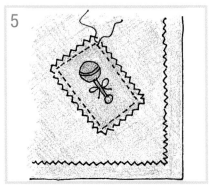

Hooded Bath Blanket

GÖTZ

Hooded bath blankets are needed to keep dolls warm after bath time. They are lots more fun when the hood is decorated with animal appliqués. The blanket shown here has a puppy dog face and ears made with brown felt. Simple embroidery and button eyes are the finishing touch.

PUPPY DOG BATH BLANKET

PUPPY DOG

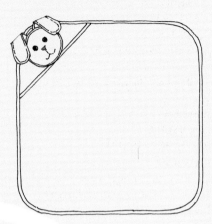

SUPPLIES

¾ yd. white terry cloth

Package of white double fold quilt binding

9" x 12" rectangle of tan felt

Dark brown thread

2 black buttons, size ½"

Scrap of black felt for the nose

Black embroidery floss

Fabric glue

CUTTING INSTRUCTIONS

From the white terry cloth, cut:
- One 24" square.
- One hood (Pattern 64).

From the tan felt, cut:
- One face (Pattern 65).
- Two ears (Pattern 67).

From the black felt, cut:
- One nose (Pattern 66).

Make a hooded bath blanket without an animal face and with a larger hood. Using the same pattern (Pattern 64), cut along the cutting line for the larger hood.

1 Round the corners of the 24" square using the hood pattern piece as a guide for each corner.

2 Open out one side of the binding and stitch to the wrong side of the diagonal edge of the hood. Cut off the excess. Fold over to the right side and stitch close to the fold. Place the hood onto one corner of the blanket and baste around the outside edge.

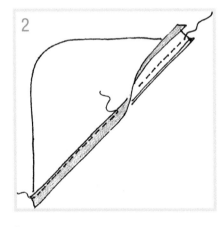

3 Using the same procedure in Step 2, bind the outside edges of the blanket with the binding, turning the end under ¼" when you come back to the start of the binding.

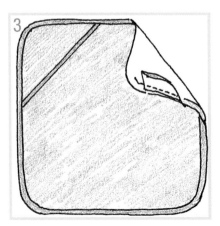

4 Stitch around the ears with dark brown thread ⅛" from the edge.

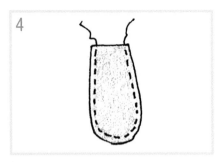

5 With two strands of embroidery floss, stitch the mouth lines with an outline stitch.

6 Glue the nose to the felt above the mouth. Sew the buttons to the face as marked on the pattern piece.

7 Stitch the face to the hood of the blanket with the dark brown thread (use white thread in the bobbin) ⅛" from the edge, tucking the straight edge of the ears under the face as marked on the pattern piece. Note that the face extends above the binding at the top and bottom of the hood.

8 Fold the ears over the face and glue in place.

Resources

Many of the fabrics and craft items can be found at larger craft and sewing stores such as Michael's®, Hancock® and Jo-Ann® stores. Dolls and accessories can be purchased from toy stores, mail order companies and retail outlets. Their Web sites will locate stores nearest you. The shoes shown in the photos can be obtained through Web sites and mail order companies.

Fancywork and Fashion
Joan Hinds
P.O. Box 3554
Duluth, MN 55803
(800) 365-5257
http://www.fancyworkandfashion.com
Sewing pattern books, accessories, doll sewing supplies including zippers, Dritz for Dolls® notions and a quarterly newsletter with patterns for 18" child dolls and occasionally for 15" baby dolls.

SHOES AND ACCESSORIES
CR's Crafts
P.O. Box 8
Leland, IA 50453
(877) 277-2782
http://www.crscraft.com

Talina's
15791 S.E. Highway 224
Clackamas, OR 97015
(800) 257-9450
http://www.dollsupply.com

DOLL SEWING NOTIONS
Sewing Notions
Prym-Dritz Corporation
(800) 255-7796 (customer service)
http://www.dritz.com
Includes Dritz for Dolls® notions

MACHINE EMBROIDERY DESIGNS
Amazing Designs
(800) 553-1691
http://www.amazingdesigns.com

Cactus Punch, Inc.
4955 N. Shamrock Pl.
Tucson, AZ 85705
(800) 933-8081
http://www.cactuspunch.com

Designs So Fine, Inc.
1311 Somerset Blvd.
St. Cloud, MN 56303
http://www.dsewfine.com

VSM Sewing, Inc.
31000 Viking Pkwy.
Westlake, OH 44145
http://www.husqvarnaviking.com

DOLL FURNITURE
Badger Basket
(800) 236-1310
http://www.badgerbasket.com

DOLLS
Adora Dolls®
Adora, Inc.
300 Columbus Circle, Suite D
Edison, NJ 08837
(877) MY-ADORA
http://www.adoradoll.com

Bitty Baby® and Bitty Twins® by Pleasant Company
8400 Fairway Pl.
P.O. Box 620190
Middleton, WI 53562-0190
(800) 845-0005
http://www.americangirl.com
Dolls, shoes and accessories available by mail order only.

Corolle Dolls
1 Corporate Dr.
Grantsville, MD 21536
(800) 628-3655
http://www.corolledolls.com

CR's Crafts
P.O. Box 8
Leland, IA 50453
(877) 277-2782
http://www.crscraft.com

Dolls by Berenguer, Inc.
9590 N.W. 40th Street Rd.
Miami, FL 33178
http://www.jctoys.com

Fisher Price® Dolls
http://www.fisher-price.com

Götz® Dolls
This doll manufacturer has recently gone out of business, but dolls are still available in various toy stores around the country

Lee Middleton Original Dolls
480 Olde Worthington Rd., Suite 110
Westerville, OH 43082
(614) 901-0604
http://www.leemiddleton.com

Martha Pullen
149 Old Big Cove Rd.
Brownsboro, AL 35741
(800) 547-4176 ext.2
http://www.marthapullen.com

Zapf Creation® Dolls
(877) 629-9273
http://www.zapf-creation.com

About the Author

Joan has written 12 sewing books for dolls since 1992. All of them have patterns and instructions for clothing and accessories for the popular 18" vinyl doll. The outfits range from today's pre-teen clothing to ball gowns and international costumes. In 1989, she and a former partner formed Fancywork and Fashion, a company that markets doll costuming and sewing books, sewing notions and accessories. A quarterly newsletter is also published that features patterns and technique tips for the popular vinyl 18" child doll with occasional patterns for 15" baby dolls.

Creating costumes and accessories for dolls is the perfect expression for Joan's love of sewing and design. All aspects of pattern drafting, fashion and interior design, embellishment and fantasy are incorporated in projects that need only small amounts of fabric and trim. As a former newborn nursery R.N., Joan was excited to work with baby dolls in her latest book, "Sew Baby Doll Clothes." It is her first book of baby doll clothing and the first book to feature multiple sizes.

Joan loves to travel the country to share her knowledge with sewing and embroidery guilds, trade shows and shops. Her work has been shown in "Designs in Machine Embroidery," "Sew Beautiful," "Doll Crafter" and "Creative Needle" magazines. She has made an appearance on the PBS series, "America Sews with Sue Hausmann." Joan and her husband Fletcher reside in Minnesota. With two grown children, they are thoroughly enjoying their empty nest.